CULTURE SMART!
TUNISIA

Gerald Zarr

·K·U·P·E·R·A·R·D·

First published in Great Britain 2009
by Kuperard, an imprint of Bravo Ltd
59 Hutton Grove, London N12 8DS
Tel: +44 (0) 20 8446 2440   Fax: +44 (0) 20 8446 2441
www.culturesmartguides.com
Inquiries: sales@kuperard.co.uk

Culture Smart! is a registered trademark of Bravo Ltd

Distributed in the United States and Canada
by Random House Distribution Services
1745 Broadway, New York, NY 10019
Tel: +1 (212) 572-2844   Fax: +1 (212) 572-4961
Inquiries: csorders@randomhouse.com

Series Editor Geoffrey Chesler
Design Bobby Birchall

ISBN 978 1 85733 477 7

British Library Cataloguing in Publication Data
A CIP catalogue entry for this book is available from the
British Library

Printed in Malaysia

Cover image: Old town, Hammamet. © *Vuk8691/Dreamstime.com*
Images on pages 15 © Andrea Nardi; 21 © David Bjorgen; 23 (top) © Patrick Giraud;
23 (bottom) © Wolfgang Sauber; 38 and 164 © elian; 56, 86, 99, 100, 105, 113 (top),
121, and 133 © Citizen59; 57 © rais58; 75 © Steve Evans; 84 and 137 © SuperManu;
91 © Tunisian Tourist Office, London; 101 © Ian Sewell; 113 (bottom) © Ranko;
114 © Tony Hisgett; 119 © Jaume Ollé; 122 © Henning Leweke; 125 © Elcéd77;
128 © DrFO.Jr.Tn; and 134 © Bertrand Bouret

About the Author

GERALD ZARR is an American writer and consultant on international development. He was born in Worcester, Massachusetts, and graduated from Clark University with high honors in international relations. He earned his JD at New York University School of Law. He then practiced law with the international law firm of Shearman & Sterling, and taught law in Liberia and at Case Western Reserve University in Cleveland, Ohio. As a senior diplomat in the US Foreign Service, he lived in Pakistan, Tunisia, Ghana, Egypt, Haiti, and Bulgaria for more than twenty years. Since retiring from the Foreign Service in 1995, Gerald Zarr has worked as an international consultant in Eastern Europe, the former Soviet Union, and the Middle East. His articles have appeared in the *International Herald Tribune*, the *Los Angeles Times*, and other publications. As an enrichment lecturer for various cruise lines, he also speaks on historical and cultural topics on Baltic, Mediterranean, Black Sea, Caribbean, Indian Ocean, and Pacific cruises.

The Culture Smart! series is continuing to expand.
For further information and latest titles visit
www.culturesmartguides.com

The publishers would like to thank **CultureSmart!**Consulting for its help in researching and developing the concept for this series.

CultureSmart!Consulting creates tailor-made seminars and consultancy programs to meet a wide range of corporate, public-sector, and individual needs. Whether delivering courses on multicultural team building in the USA, preparing Chinese engineers for a posting in Europe, training call-center staff in India, or raising the awareness of police forces to the needs of diverse ethnic communities, it provides essential, practical, and powerful skills worldwide to an increasingly international workforce.

For details, visit www.culturesmartconsulting.com

CultureSmart!Consulting and **CultureSmart!** guides have both contributed to and featured regularly in the weekly travel program "Fast Track" on BBC World TV.

contents

contents

Map of Tunisia

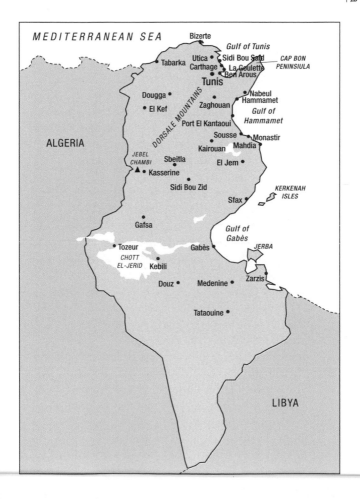

introduction

Sitting at the northernmost bulge of North Africa and thrusting toward Europe, Tunisia is Africa at its most Mediterranean and Arabia at its most cosmopolitan. These comparisons are appropriate, because from its earliest days Tunisia has been open to influences from abroad. All the great empires of the Mediterranean basin have ruled Tunisia, leaving fascinating vestiges of their rule. Africa—the Roman name for Tunisia—eventually came to describe the immense continent beyond its borders. Then Islam's conquering armies drew the country within the Arab sphere of influence, where it remains.

Tunisia has more than eight hundred miles of coastline, cork oak forests and rolling mountains, and in the south, the salt lakes and seemingly alien architecture of the desert that were transformed into the planet Tatooine in the *Star Wars* films.

Tunis is a bustling Mediterranean metropolis of nearly two million people. The narrow streets of its medieval *medina* are crammed with vendors of antiques, jewelry, pottery, carpets, books, perfumes, dried fruit, and spices. A mere ten miles away lie the remains of the Phoenician and Roman city of Carthage—a treasure trove for the history buff.

Unlike its neighbors, Tunisia is not oil-rich, so it must rely on the skills and entrepreneurial spirit of all of its people to make its way in the world. Women play a role in national development that is scarcely equaled in any other Arab country.

This book explores the codes and paradoxes of Tunisian life—a North African country that looks to France and Italy as its reference points, but remains determinedly Arab and Muslim. Tunisians are warm and hospitable, but for the uninitiated there can be pitfalls galore in social interaction. Candor and honesty are not valued as highly as respect, dignity, and avoiding stigma.

The Tunisia that visitors tend to see is modern, progressive, and prosperous; but many traditionally minded people still believe in the power of blessings and curses, explain difficult times as *maktoub* (fate), and view illness as the result of maliciously intended magic.

Culture Smart! Tunisia aims to start you on the path to understanding this complex, rich, and fascinating culture by opening a window into the private lives of Tunisians, to show how they behave at home and how they react to foreign visitors. The brief historical overview provides an insight into the way the past has helped to shape the Tunisian present. There are chapters on customs and traditions, with advice on how to make friends and avoid faux pas. For the business traveler, there is practical guidance on how to get things done, and how to make the most of the opportunities that present themselves.

Culture Smart! Tunisia seeks to make your trip as rich as possible, to take you beyond the clichés to the real people. Welcome to Tunisia. *Marhaba!*

Key Facts

Official Name	Al Jumhuriyyah at-Tunisiyyah	Tunisia is an associate member of the European Union.
Capital City	Tunis (population approx. 1.8 million)	
Other Cities	Sfax (pop. 281,000), Nabeul, Gabès, Sousse, Kairouan, Bizerte	
Population	Approx. 10.3 million	
Area	63,170 sq. miles (164,000 sq. km approx.)	
Geography	Situated at the northernmost bulge of central North Africa. Its neighbors are Algeria and Libya.	
Terrain	Dorsale mountain range across north central part of country; fertile northern and central coastal plain; semiarid central plateau; desert in south	
Climate	Varies greatly. Three general climates: Mediterranean (mild, wet winters, hot summers); Dorsale mountains (cold, wet winters, occasional snow, hot summers); desert (hot with little rain, cold nighttime temperatures)	
Natural Resources	Phosphates, salt, iron ore, natural gas, crude oil	

Language	Tunisian Arabic (Tunsi)	Modern Standard Arabic is is spoken. French is also used in literature and the media.
Religion	98 percent Sunni Muslim	Other religions: Christianity, Judaism
Government	Republic	Executive power is in the hands of a strong president.
Currency	Tunisian Dinar (TD)	Plans are under way to make the dinar fully convertible.
Media	There are both private and state-run radio stations. There are a few regular TV and four satellite TV channels.	National newspapers are available in French and Arabic. The weekly *Tunis News* is the only English-language newspaper. International papers and magazines in English are available.
Electricity	220 volts (50 Hz)	Two-prong European plugs are used.
DVD/Video	SECAM system	
Telephone	Tunisia's country code is 216	To dial out, dial 00 followed by the country code.
Internet Domain	.tn	
Time Zone	One hour ahead of GMT. Two hours ahead from April to October	

chapter one

LAND & PEOPLE

Tunisia, Morocco, and Algeria are the three westernmost countries of the Arab world, and are collectively known as the Maghreb (meaning "the West" in Arabic).

With an area of 63,170 square miles (163,610 sq. km), Tunisia is the smallest country in North Africa. It is also the most cohesive: almost all of its ten million people speak Arabic, and the population is almost entirely Muslim. A single major city, Tunis, gave its name to the country, and dominates the land politically and culturally. No other Tunisian city comes close to it in size.

GEOGRAPHY

Tunisia is situated on the Mediterranean coast of North Africa, midway between the Atlantic Ocean and the Nile Valley, and only ninety miles from Sicily. It is bordered by Algeria in the west and Libya in the southeast. An abrupt southern turn gives Tunisia two faces on the Mediterranean and a shoreline of more than 800 miles (1,300 km).

Despite its relatively small size, Tunisia has great diversity in geography and climate. The Dorsale, an extension of the Atlas Mountains, traverses Tunisia in a northeasterly direction from the Algerian border in the west to the Cape Bon Peninsula. North of the Dorsale is the Tell, a region characterized by low, rolling hills and plains, except for the forested mountains of the northwest. Along Tunisia's eastern Mediterranean coast is a plain known as the Sahil, famous for its olive monoculture. Inland from here, and south of the Dorsale, is the semiarid central plateau, fit mainly for livestock grazing. Further south lies the sea of sands of the Sahara.

The highest peak is Jebel Chambi at 5,050 feet (1,544 m) near Kasserine. The only permanent river is the Medjerda, which rises in eastern Algeria and flows through the country to the sea.

Many of Tunisia's drainage systems end in *chotts* (saline lakes) in the south. The largest of these is the Chott el-Jerid, which is dry during half the year but forms a shallow salt lake during the winter months. Along the Sahara's northern perimeter are oasis towns with extensive *palmeraies* (palm groves) fed by artesian springs, producing choice dates. These towns include Tozeur, with a large

tourist zone and ample creature comforts, Kebili, noted for its hot springs, and Douz, the most traveled gateway into the Sahara.

In the mid-1970s Tunisia became more urban than rural. Currently, more than 60 percent of the population live in cities and towns. The largest city is Tunis, with nearly two million people. The next largest is Sfax (population 281,000), an industrial city and port on the Gulf of Gabès. Then come a clump of large towns—Nabeul, Sousse, Kairouan, Gabès, and Bizerte—all within the 100,000 to 200,000 population range. Except for Kairouan, all these towns are on the coast.

CLIMATE

Three main natural features affect Tunisia's climate: the moderating influences of the Mediterranean Sea, the Dorsale range, which blocks the northern rains from reaching the south, and the Sahara, with its hot, dry sirocco winds that blow northward over much of the country during the summer.

Northern Tunisia has a Mediterranean climate, with hot, dry summers (June to September) and wet winters (November to March). In the north rainfall averages around 20 inches (50 cm) a year, with heavier rain and even snow in the forested mountains of the northwest, and the winter nights are damp and chilly.

Central Tunisia comes alive in spring with spectacular displays of wildflowers, but the summers are very hot and everything quickly turns to brown. Winters, particularly at higher elevations, can be cold and bleak.

In the south, rainfall is negligible and the weather remains hot year-round. At night there are dramatic drops in temperature.

THE PEOPLE

It is not clear who were the original inhabitants of the area we now know as Tunisia. We do know, however, that by the time the Phoenicians arrived, *c.* 100 BCE, the country was already occupied by North Africa's indigenous people—the Berbers. Of stocky physique with a high incidence of light hair and blue eyes, the Berbers are Caucasians akin to other Mediterranean peoples. Horses, which arrived in North Africa around 1200 BCE, became an integral part of the Berber identity and enabled the Berbers to dominate their environment. The name "Berber" originates from the Greek word for foreigners, *barbaroi,* meaning those who live outside civilization. The Berbers' own name for themselves was much loftier; in their own language they called themselves "the noble ones" (*imiazen*—singular, *amazigh*).

The Arab conquests of the seventh and eleventh centuries brought a different physique and colouring to Tunisia. Gradually the Arab–Berber mélange became dispersed over the country, though subtle distinctions are discernible; where this is the case the coastal and northern peoples tend to the stocky

Berber type, and those of the inland and southern regions, where Arab concentration was highest, are more slender and darker-skinned, with darker eyes and hair.

Today most Tunisians claim Arab ancestry, speak Arabic, and find only traces of Berber culture in their lives. In this sense Tunisia contrasts with Morocco and Algeria, where the Berbers are still substantial minorities.

Since the end of the last Arab invasion the ethnic composition of the population has changed little. Black Africans, once widely used as household slaves and concubines, have affected the composition of the population only slightly, although skin color ranges from bronze to black in the southern oases.

During the period of the Catholic *reconquista*, Muslim refugees from Spain sought asylum and were welcomed in Tunisia. This migration lasted for centuries, culminating in the fall of Granada, the last independent Muslim kingdom, in 1492. In all, some 200,000 Spanish Muslims settled in Tunis, the Medjerda Valley, and on the Sharik Peninsula in the north, bringing with them their urban culture and advanced agricultural and irrigation techniques.

There was also a large infusion of Sephardic Jews from Spain at that time. In 1948, the Jewish population of Tunisia was 105,000. Since then, the number of Jews has steadily declined. Many Jews left when Tunisia became independent in 1956. During the 1967 Arab–Israeli War, Jews were attacked by Arab mobs, and synagogues and shops were burned. The government denounced the violence, and President Habib Bourguiba apologized to the Chief Rabbi. The government appealed to the Jewish population to stay, but did not bar them from leaving. Subsequently, 7,000 Jews left for France. Today an estimated 1,500 Jews remain, mainly living in Tunis, Jerba, and Zarzis.

During the Ottoman period, from the sixteenth to the nineteenth century, intermarriage between Tunisians and Turks, Greeks, Circassians, and other subject people of the Ottoman Empire had a significant social and commercial impact, but did little to alter the Arab–Berber mix.

The country's ethnic diversity is evident in the great variety of Tunisian family names.

A BRIEF HISTORY

Tunisia's strategic position has ensured it an eventful history. Phoenicians, Romans, Vandals, Byzantines, Arabs, Ottomans, and French have all occupied it at one time or another.

Phoenicians (1100 BCE–146 CE)

The Phoenician ships must have startled the Berber shepherds watching from the shore at the time of that first visit around the year 1100 BCE. They came from Phoenicia, a loose confederation of maritime trading city-states (including Aradus, Beirut, Byblos, Sidon, and Tyre) strung out along the coast of modern-day Syria, Lebanon, and Israel. They were first drawn to the North African coast in their search for a rest stop between their home cities and the port of Gadès (now Cadiz) that they built in southern Spain. They needed a halfway point where they could service, supply, and shelter their ships, and safely spend the winter. So they came to present-day Tunisia and founded Utica as the first in a chain of trading posts that eventually included Bizerte, Sousse, Monastir, and Sfax. Nearly every port of consequence in southern Europe and North Africa today was founded by the Phoenicians in antiquity.

Tunisia was home to the greatest of their settlements, Kart Hadasht ("new city" in the Punic, or Phoenician, language), which we call Carthage. According to legend, it was founded in 814 BCE by a princess of Tyre known to Western readers as Dido.

The Founding of Carthage

Virgil's Aeneid relates that the Berber chieftain would sell Dido only as much land for her new city as could be covered by a single ox hide. Dido had the hide cut into the thinnest of strips, which she used to surround the hill that became the center of Carthage. That hill is named Byrsa, meaning "ox hide" in Greek.

After Phoenicia fell under Persian domination in 539 BCE, its western colonies looked to Carthage for leadership. Carthage grew into the great metropolis of the Phoenician world, its wealth and trading craft protected by a powerful navy.

By the fourth century BCE, Carthage had carved out territory, similar in extent to modern-day Tunisia, that stretched from Tabarka in the northwest to Sfax in the southeast. This included the fertile lands of the Cap Bon Peninsula and the Medjerda Valley, which supplied Carthage with a large and exportable agricultural surplus.

It was inevitable that this regional primacy would lead to conflict with the other great powers of the Mediterranean: first Greece, and then Rome. Carthage fought numerous wars with the Greeks over Sicily, which it finally conquered in the middle of the third century BCE.

This set the stage for three wars between Rome and Carthage (the "Punic Wars") that would preoccupy the two powers for the next century. Rome launched the first war in 264 BCE with a campaign to win control of Sicily. Roman successes on land balanced by the supremacy of Carthage's navy at sea led to a stalemate that dragged on for twenty years. Finally, Carthage sued for peace, gave up Sicily plus Corsica and Sardinia, and paid a war indemnity.

The great Carthaginian general Hannibal Barca came within a whisker of crushing the emerging Roman Empire in the Second Punic War (218–202 BCE). Carthage struck the first blow after evidence of Rome's war preparations had become unmistakable. Hannibal set off from Spain at the head of an army said to have numbered 90,000 infantrymen backed by 12,000 cavalry and thirty-seven elephants. Hannibal's journey took him across hostile Gaul (modern-day southern France) before an epic crossing of the Alps that saw him descend into the plains of northern Italy in the spring of 217 BCE.

Hannibal remained in Italy for sixteen years, defeating every army that the Romans threw against him, but his goal—the capture of Rome itself—eluded him. Rome eventually gained the upper hand by cutting off his reinforcements, bringing the war to Africa, and forcing him to abandon Italy. In 202 BCE, the Romans, under Scipio Africanus, defeated Hannibal at Zama (present-day Sidi Youssef)—one of the ancient world's most decisive battles, because it ended the Carthaginian Empire.

Hannibal escaped east to the mother-city of Tyre, where he initially received a hero's welcome; but he eventually ran out of patrons willing to incur the anger of Rome by sheltering him. As the Roman vise tightened around him, he took his own life in 182 BCE.

Hannibal and the Tunisian Connection

To promote its international name recognition, Tunisia has identified itself closely with the great Carthaginian general. The Hannibal Club is a global network of local chapters in Asia, Europe, and North America that aims to broaden Tunisia's cultural and economic links with the world. Hannibal remains a hero to Tunisians, his name appearing on numerous streets and cafés throughout the country. A $3-million memorial to him is being built in Carthage.

Historians have long debated why Rome chose to attack and destroy Carthage after it had been brought to its knees and posed no discernible threat. But the Roman senator Cato fanned the war fury against Carthage through his oft-repeated words "*Delenda est Carthago*" ("Carthage must be destroyed"), and the Roman Republic obliged. In the one-sided Third Punic War (149–146 BCE), Rome finished off its one-time rival. Not even the smoldering walls of Carthage, saturated with the blood of the slain, were allowed to stand. Its population was dispersed, the city razed to the ground, and its earth sown with salt.

The Roman Period (146 BCE – 439 CE)
Rome began to regret its treatment of Carthage a century later when it was struck with a nasty patch of civil strife, which, the people believed, was due to the mother goddess Ceres punishing Rome for the obliteration of Carthage. So Rome decided to rebuild the city. In 46 BCE—exactly one century after the destruction—Julius  Caesar had a detailed street layout prepared for Carthage, but he was assassinated before the work was carried out. His grand-nephew Augustus completed the restoration and piously dedicated a new shrine to Ceres in Carthage. From that time onward, the goddess' emblematic sheaf appeared

on the city's coins and her spring festival became the city's premier event.

Not only did the Romans return to Carthage, but they stayed for more than five hundred years. Under the governorship of a praetor or proconsul, Carthage became the capital of a new Roman province named "Africa." The province at first occupied the northeastern third of modern Tunisia. As the boundaries of Roman rule were extended east and west along the continent's north coast, the word "Africa" came to refer to an ever larger area— and eventually encompassed the entire continent.

The province was peaceful and prosperous. By the first century CE, the wheat-growing plains of the Medjerda Valley and the Tell Plateau were supplying more than 60 percent of the Roman Empire's grain requirements. More olive oil was produced in Tunisia than in Italy, and almost as much wine.

The province of Africa attracted settlers from all over the Empire. Veterans in early retirement settled on farming plots promised for their military service. A sizable Latin-speaking population grew alongside the Berber and Punic speakers.

Speaking Punic

Under Roman rule, an educated Carthaginian might read literature and philosophy in Greek, use Latin in the law courts, and speak Punic at home. Visiting her brother in Rome, Septimius Severus's sister spoke Punic and little else. Punic survived in outlying areas to the fifth century, according to St. Augustine.

Rome's imprint throughout North Africa was immense, building more than two hundred cities and constructing thousands of miles of roads with mileposts marking every 1,000 paces. Stately public buildings as high as seven stories, bridges, dams, irrigation systems, temples, baths, and aristocratic homes were added. An aqueduct near Zaghouan carried 8.5 million gallons of water daily to Carthage. By the end of the second century, no fewer than 15 percent of Rome's senators came from present-day Tunisia.

The apex of North African influence in Rome occurred under Septimius Severus, the first North African to ascend the throne of the Caesars. He was born in 145 CE into a wealthy and distinguished family of Phoenician lineage. Although he came to power by force, he was the strong, able ruler that Rome desperately needed. His eighteen-year reign (193–211) marks the high tide of the Roman Empire as an enlightened pagan state. The brilliance of his reign is evidenced by the baths of Caracalla and the Severan arches in the Roman Forum and his hometown of Leptis Magna in present-day Libya. Roman sites in Tunisia are replete with architectural gems built by Septimius Severus.

The Fossa Regia

The Romans dug a huge demarcation border ditch—in Latin, the *fossa regia*—from Tabarka on the northwest coast to south of Sfax on the Gulf of Gabès. Some historians contrast the success of lands within the *fossa regia* with the often chaotic history of countries beyond the ditch, suggesting that Tunisia's modern success can be traced back to its Carthaginian and Roman roots.

After his dynasty ran out in 235, Rome was rocked by a half century of military anarchy. In this span, twenty-eight soldiers were proclaimed emperor, only one of whom died before he could be deposed. Imperial statues were cast with replaceable heads so that official portraiture could keep pace with the bloody succession of soldier-emperors.

This anarchy spawned rampant inflation and crushing taxation that were devastating to the lives of ordinary Romans. Desperately, they sought relief from their personal and societal woes and found it in Christianity, which spread rapidly in the third century. Entering through its polyglot port cities, North Africa's first Christian communities were established at Carthage.

Not surprisingly, the anarchy and the increasing bankruptcy of imperial Rome led the authorities to a renewed wave of official persecutions against Christians. One of the most noted was the trial and execution of Bishop (later St.) Cyprian of Carthage in 258. The scion of a wealthy and distinguished pagan family, Cyprian had been a barrister at the law courts and a professor of rhetoric at the university of Carthage before his elevation to the priesthood. As bishop, he was devoted to pastoral care and church unity as evidenced by some sixty of his letters to his flock and fellow churchmen that survive.

Eighty-seven bishops responded to Cyprian's call to attend a regional council held covertly at Carthage in 256, following which he was arrested. The Roman proconsul treated him with great deference and courtesy, but he was convicted nonetheless, and sentenced to death. Cyprian reciprocated the judge's respectful behavior but held firm to his faith. Cyprian's execution, witnessed by a large crowd of his supporters, was held in the grounds of his villa in Carthage.

In 313, Emperor Constantine announced toleration for Christianity in the Edict of Milan, and later became the first Roman emperor to embrace Christianity. In 324, he announced the moving of his capital to the eastern city of Byzantium, which he renamed New Rome.

By the beginning of the fifth century, Roman power was in terminal decline and a new force was about to be unleashed against Rome.

The Vandals (439–533)

In 406, the Germanic Vandals stormed over the frozen Rhine to escape the Huns to their east, and pillaged through Gaul. They crossed the Pyrenees and by 409 had settled in southern Spain, the region we now call Andalusia—the name derived from the Arabic for "Land of the Vandals."

In 429, the Vandals' vigorous new leader, Genseric, led the entire Vandal nation, a total of

80,000 men, women, and children, across the straits of Gibraltar, to North Africa, one of history's most astonishing invasions. The Vandals marched eastward along the coast, closely supported by their fleet, pillaging and looting as they went. A year later, they reached the Roman city of Hippo Regius (now Annaba) in Algeria. Bishop Augustine of Hippo lay dying within its walls. The Vandals besieged and conquered the city, destroying everything except for Augustine's cathedral and library, which they left untouched.

After a halt of several years in Algeria, the Vandals resumed their eastward march. In 439 they took Carthage and made it their capital. As an indication of how far the Roman Empire had fallen since its heyday, the city was taken without a fight, while most of the inhabitants were attending races at the hippodrome.

The Vandals expelled the Romans, seized their sumptuous estates, and took quickly to their new

SAINT AUGUSTINE
The most famous North African Christian
was St. Augustine, who was born in 354 CE to
Berber parents in present-day Souk Ahras,
Algeria. His mother, St. Monica, brought him
up as a Christian, but he gave up his religion
on going to school at Carthage. There he
became adept at rhetoric. In his *Confessions*
he repents of his wild youth in Carthage,
where he had an illegitimate son. In 384, he
went to Milan to teach, coming under the
influence of St. Ambrose, Bishop of Milan,
and this became the most critical period of
his life. He was baptized on Easter Day in the
year 387. After five years he returned to North
Africa, where he became a famous preacher
and later Bishop of Hippo. More than 350 of
his preserved sermons are believed to be
authentic. *The City of God* is one of his best-
known books. He died in 430, during the
Vandal siege.

aristocratic lifestyle. They aped the Romans in their
dress, their pastimes, and their conspicuous
consumption. They restored Roman baths, theaters,
and churches, and adopted the written Latin
language even though most of them were illiterate.

During his long and successful rule Genseric
transformed himself from war leader to hereditary
king, but his successors were not able to maintain
his warrior zeal under the hot African sun.

Byzantine Rule (533–693)

The Byzantine Emperor Justinian, ensconced in his brilliant capital of Constantinople, was pleased by how successfully he had revived the fortunes of the eastern half of the Roman Empire. Now he had to do the same for the western half. He dispatched his best general, Flavius Belisarius, with a fleet  of 500 ships and an army of 16,000 men to take Carthage and root out the Vandals.

The expedition arrived while the Vandal fleet was in Sardinia and the army away on maneuvers, so Belisarius was able to march unopposed up the coast. He defeated a Vandal force ten miles outside the city walls, and entered Carthage propitiously on St. Cyprian's name day; but the Vandal army returned at that precise moment, trapping the Byzantine army inside the city. Belisarius responded by ordering an unexpected cavalry charge out of the city gates, which broke the Vandal siege, the Vandal army, and Vandal rule over North Africa in a single sally.

The Vandals were expelled from North Africa. Vandal men were enslaved or taken into the Byzantine army, while many of the captured Vandal women were taken as wives by Byzantine soldiers. The best Vandal warriors were formed into five cavalry regiments, known as *Vandali Iustiniani* (Justinian's Vandals), and stationed on the Persian frontier. Gelimer, the last Vandal king, was honorably treated by Justinian and received large estates in Anatolia.

For over a century, the Byzantines ruled North Africa from Carthage with comparative ease. A viceroy, or exarch, exercised civil and military authority there, and enjoyed considerable autonomy from Constantinople.

Not content with his subordinate role, however, the Exarch Gregory declared himself independent of Constantinople in 647. This was terrible timing, because in that very year the first Arab armies of conquest penetrated Tunisia. The culture, religion, language, and literature of the country, and even its capital, were about to change.

The Arab Conquest (647–701)

The armies flying the green banner of the new religion of Islam swept out of Arabia and conquered Egypt by 640—only eight years after the death of Mohammed. It took much longer for the Arabs to subdue present-day Tunisia. They were opposed by two formidable powers— Byzantium and the Berber tribes. Byzantine power was based on the fortified coastal cities protected by the imperial navy, while the Berber tribesmen were superb horsemen and the full military equal of the Arabs.

As the Arab armies neared, the Exarch Gregory began to appreciate the extent of the threat he faced. In 647, he moved his army south from Carthage to Sufetula (present-day Sbeitla), so that he could face the Arab attack with the support of his Berber allies. A hundred thousand Berbers and the Byzantine army met the Arab onslaught at

Sufetula, but were overwhelmed, and Gregory died on the field of battle. Yet the Byzantine navy still controlled the seas, and it was not until 698 that Carthage fell to the Arabs.

The Berbers—up to this point Christian with a Jewish and pagan minority—had a strong affinity for Islam, but bristled at the idea of Arab rule. The legendary Berber princess Al-Kahina defeated the Arabs at Tebessa in Algeria in 696, but was eventually cornered and killed at the Roman amphitheater in El-Jem (about 100 miles from Tunis) in the year 701.

Local Islamic Dynasties (702–99)

After the Arab conquest, "Ifriqiya"—as the Arabs referred to Rome's province of Africa—was governed by a succession of local emirs (commanders) under the authority of the caliph in Damascus and, after 750, the caliph in Baghdad. Tunisia was too distant from these great power centers to be subjected to direct rule. Instead, a succession of local Islamic dynasties, both Berber and Arab, competed for power in Ifriqiya.

Aghlabids (800–909)

In 800, the Abbasid Caliph Harun al-Rashid—whose magnificent Baghdad court may have inspired *The Thousand and One Nights*—appointed Ibrahim ibn al-Aghlab as hereditary emir of Ifriqiya. The Aghlabids—nominally vassals of the Abbasids—ruled Tunisia for over a century, leaving the country with its most enduring architectural legacies. The Great Mosque in Kairouan and the *ribat* (forts) at Sousse and

Monastir were all built during the Aghlabid period, often referred to as Ifriqiya's "golden age." Ifriqiya once more became

prosperous from agriculture as the Aghlabids rebuilt and added to the Roman irrigation system.

The Fatimids (909–1049)

The Berbers continued to chafe under Arab rule. In the early years of the tenth century, a militant group of Berber Shiites known as the Fatimids (named for Fatima, Mohammed's daughter) launched a holy war against the Sunni Arab Aghlabids. The Fatimids were victorious and installed their leader, Ubaidullah Said, who was declared to be the *mahdi* or "divinely guided one," as ruler over a great swath of North African territory. In honor of the *mahdi*, the Fatimids built the new capital of Mahdia on an easily defended coastal headland; but they did not stay there long. In 969, they invaded Egypt and built another new capital, this one named *al-Qahira* (The Victorious), which we know as Cairo.

Fatimid rule lasted in Tunisia until 1049, when their Berber vassals (known as Zirids) broke their ties with their overlords in Cairo, formally rejected Shi'ism, and returned to the Sunni fold. Anti-Shiite riots swept through the cities and towns of Tunisia, resulting in many deaths, effectively marking the end of Shiite rule in Tunisia.

The Children of the Moon

The Fatimid caliph, sitting in his palace in Cairo, fumed over the news from Tunisia. He resolved to wreak havoc on the perfidious Zirids and devised an ingenious punishment: he would eternally damn them with the plague of the *Beni Hilal*.

The *Beni Hilal*, or Children of the Moon, was an anarchic community living in the Egyptian desert, descended from Arab Bedouin clans that had migrated to Egypt after the first Muslim conquest. As their numbers had swelled, perhaps to a quarter of a million strong, they had become more assertive. Not even the Fatimid caliph dared test the loyalty of his army against the 50,000 young warriors that the clan chiefs could lead into battle. So instead of risking battle, the caliph came up with a brilliant alternate strategy. Through a series of flattering audiences with the clan chiefs, he persuaded the *Beni Hilal* to pick up stakes and go to Tunisia.

In 1051 the great nomad horde migrated west. They brushed aside the Zirid army and spread over the region, in the words of the historian Ibn Khaldun, like a "swarm of locusts." They destroyed towns and cities, impoverishing the land. Their livestock turned the Berbers' rich farmland into pasturage and, eventually, steppe.

Zirid Tunisia (1049–1135)

The Zirid emir tried to reason with the *Beni Hilal*—to come to some accommodation with them—but it was impossible. The clans held an official land grant from the Fatimid caliph—and all they wanted was to be left alone to enjoy their nomadic lifestyle.

Finally, to escape the *Beni Hilal*, the Zirids moved as far away as they could without leaving Tunisia. They fortified and occupied the coastal citadel of Mahdia. For almost a century, Mahdia became the Zirid trading hub and home port for their navy. Their control over the countryside was negligible.

Norman–Sicilian Occupation (1135–60)
In the first half of the twelfth century, Roger II, the Norman king of Sicily, attacked Zirid Tunisia. The Normans had initially come to southern Italy as mercenaries in the service of various Italian warlords, but before long realized it was more fun to wield power for themselves. They took the island of Jerba, established garrisons in Tunis, Tripoli, Gabès, and Sfax, and finally overran the Zirid capital of Mahdia in 1154.

ROGER II OF SICILY

This enlightened monarch is noted for his encouragement of Muslim scholarship and for the translations he commissioned for his trilingual court where Arabic, Greek, and Latin were all spoken. The most notable of these translations was the *Nuzhat al-Mushtaq fi Ikhtiraq Al-Afaq*, or "The Delight of One Who Wishes to Traverse the Regions of the World" by Al-Idrisi, popularly known as "The Book of Roger," which remains a prime source for twelfth-century North Africa.

Unlike his Viking slash-and-burn ancestors, Roger II was celebrated for his enlightened leadership. He welcomed the learned, and he practiced toleration toward the polyglot creeds and races of his realm. To administer his domain he hired many Arabs and Greeks, such as George of Antioch, the Zirid fleet's erstwhile *emir al bahr* (from which the English word "admiral" derives).

The Almohads (1160–1207)
The Almohads, like the Almoravids who ruled before them, were a strictly orthodox Berber Sunni sect centered in the Moroccan city of Marrakech. Between them, they ruled the Maghreb and Islamic Spain for two hundred years. The Almoravids never extended their rule to Tunisia, but the Almohads did, much to the discomfort of the Normans.

In 1160 the Almohad army and navy swept eastward across the Maghreb and forced the withdrawal of the Normans—with safe passage— from their strongholds in Ifriqiya, which was added to the Almohad Empire.

The Hafsids (1207–1574)
Mohammed Abu Hafs was a direct descendant of one of the Berber founders of the Almohad dynasty, which gave him enough cachet to be declared sultan and caliph of Ifriqiya. In 1207, he established a hereditary dynasty that ruled in Tunisia for more than three hundred years. His grandson, the poet-prince Abu Zakariya al Hafs (1228–49), moved the capital from Kairouan to Tunis, which ever since has been the political and cultural center of the country.

In 1270, Louis IX of France (St. Louis) began his ill-fated Eighth Crusade in Tunisia, a seemingly odd choice for a crusade because the Hafsid sultans were not the holy war type. They were engaged in trade and commerce, quite cosmopolitan, and on extremely good terms with many European states. But Louis didn't get very far with his crusade: he died on the beach in Carthage and the

crusade fizzled out. Before his death, he fell under the spell of the hilltop town of Sidi Bou Said, which has charmed generations of tourists ever since.

After the fall of Almohad Seville in 1248, many Muslim families left Spain and settled in Tunis, including the forebears of the great Muslim historian Ibn Khaldoun. Under Hafsid rule, Tunis became one of the grandest cities in the Islamic world, with a population of about 100,000.

By the sixteenth century, Tunisia's internal politics had become quite muddled, with ministates run by religious zealots (*marabouts*) jousting for influence with renegade Greek pirates controlling coastal enclaves. But worse was to come. In 1534, Tunis fell to the Ottoman Turks.

The Hafsid Sultan, Mulai Hassan, sought refuge in Catholic Spain—an odd choice for a Muslim ruler. But he wanted his throne back, and he

IBN KHALDOUN

Ibn Khaldoun was a historian, scholar, and statesman born into an upper-class Andalusian family in Tunis in 1332. Much is known about him from his autobiography. His *Muqaddimah* (Introduction to History), which explores the recurrent nature of historical cycles, is his best-known work. His fame spread through Europe and the Muslim world. Once, when he was on a diplomatic mission to Castile, the Spanish king offered him the return of his family's ancestral possessions if he remained. He politely declined. He died in Cairo in 1406.

realized that only Charles V, the Habsburg king-emperor, could do that for him. Charles V happily obliged. He personally led a naval expedition to recapture Tunis and put Mulai Hassan back on his throne. This victory is depicted in nine huge tapestries of Charles V's Conquest of Tunis—one of the premier works of art of the sixteenth century—on display in the Royal Palace of Madrid. Protected by a large Spanish garrison at La Goulette, the harbor of Tunis, the Hafsids became the Muslim ally of Catholic Spain in its struggle with the Turks for supremacy in the Mediterranean.

For nearly forty years the seesaw struggle raged until the Turks, with a large armada and 40,000 troops, took Tunis for the last time. The Spanish were driven out and the remnants of Hafsid rule eliminated.

Ottoman Deys, Beys, and Pashas (1574–1705)
The administration of Tunisia was at first
entrusted to the Ottoman military. An officer, or
dey, commanded each one hundred soldiers, and
a military council, or *diwan-al-asker*, composed of
all the deys, met periodically. From this council
was chosen the overall military commander, also
called a dey, who ran the country as a whole.

This arrangement lasted through the
seventeenth century, when the
civil authority of the dey was
challenged by a new official,
the *bey*, or provincial governor.
His job was to bring nomad
tribes to heel, collect taxes from
the countryside, and oversee
public works. This jockeying
between deys and beys—and
the occasional *pasha*, or
governor, who was sent out
from Istanbul—was done
without disturbing any of the

outward forms of loyalty to the Ottoman sultan.

The system worked well enough and the
country went through an undeniable period of
prosperity. Tunis was rebuilt, ancient mosques
were restored, and new aqueducts, dams,
fortresses, and bridges constructed. Muslim
refugees from Andalusia expelled by the Catholic
kings were welcomed with grants of land and a
three-year tax holiday. The refugees brought with
them a new trade of making the *chechia*, the
distinctive red felt cap of Andalusia, whose
vestiges we see today in the *Souq des Chechias* in

the *medina* of Tunis. This characteristic piece of headgear, so useful for winding a turban on,

 became an important source of revenue for Tunis. Also the ceramics industry took off, blending Ottoman, Berber, and Andalusian influences. This artistry soon became apparent in the elegant new barracks, *medersas* (schools), and mosques rising everywhere in Tunis.

Husseinite Beys of Tunis (1705–1957)
In 1705, Hussein ibn Ali Turki, whose father was Turkish and mother Tunisian, staged a coup and founded a dynasty that ruled Tunisia until 1957. This was not a linear father-to-son succession; instead, the Husseinite prince regarded as best qualified to rule was designated heir apparent during the lifetime of the reigning bey. A number of strong, capable rulers such as Bey Ali II (1756–82) and his successor Bey Hammuda (1782–1814) emerged from this selection process.

Although tied by bonds of tradition and respect to the Ottoman Sultan, the bey was independent in all but name. The ruling bey would, with sumptuous gifts, petition Istanbul for the title of pasha, which honor was invariably given. In return the beys continued to recruit Turkish soldiers for their army and received a quota of *mamluk* slave boys (recruited mainly

THE BARBARY PIRATES

Until the early nineteenth century, booty, ransom, and slaves acquired from attacks on Mediterranean towns and shipping were the major source of revenue for the beys of Tripoli, Tunis, Algeria, and Morocco. Countries that traded in the Mediterranean at first opted to pay tribute rather than incur the expense of rooting out the pirates, but eventually decided to resist. From 1801 to 1805, the United States fought its first foreign war against the Barbary pirates. In 1818, the European Congress of Aix-la-Chapelle issued an ultimatum that forced the Bey of Tunis to agree to give up piracy. An exclamation point was added to this agreement in 1827 when the Tunisian fleet was destroyed at the Battle of Navarino, having been sent there in the vain hope of helping the Ottomans put down the Greek rebellion.

from the Christian territories of the empire) who were trained as bureaucrats and gendarmerie leaders. Unlike the Turkish deys, who lived in barracks in the center of Tunis, the beys moved their court to secluded palaces. The Bardo Palace held all the instruments of state: the main army barracks, artillery depot, treasury, council chamber, and the *mamluk* secretariat.

All this changed in 1830. France seized Algeria, and five years later the Ottoman Sultan deposed the Libyan ruling dynasty and reestablished direct rule. This meant that Tunisia was surrounded by two larger powers—France and the Ottoman Empire—with designs on its territory. From that time until the establishment of the French protectorate in 1881, Tunisian rulers had to walk a political tightrope.

Ahmad Bey (1837–55) was an avowed modernizer and reformer. He abolished slavery and integrated Arabic-speaking native Tunisians into the government, which had long been dominated by the Turkish-speaking *mamluk* class. The next bey, Muhammad (1855–9), sought to unravel Ahmad's reforms. He restored slavery, claiming it was an inseparable part of Muslim society.

The final collapse of the Tunisian *beylik* came during the reign of the next bey, Muhammad al-Sadiq (1859–82). He saw the need for reform, but was too weak to implement it while keeping the European powers at bay. In 1861, he proclaimed the first constitution (*destour*) in the Arabic-speaking world, but it was suspended in 1864 during the country's financial woes. The country was hit by inflation and runaway debt, mainly due to corrupt and extortionate foreign loans pressed upon the beys by European bankers. The government responded by trying to squeeze more taxes out of the hard-pressed peasantry, who rose in revolt. The regime was nearly overthrown but ultimately suppressed the revolt through guile and brutality. Tunisia became bankrupt in 1869 and had to endure the indignity of an international financial commission, dominated by Britain, France, and Italy, being imposed upon the country.

One last attempt at reform was made during the premiership of Khereddine Pasha (1873–7), one of the most effective statesmen of the nineteenth-century Muslim world. However, his enemies within Tunisia and European intrigues outside combined to force him from office.

KHEREDDINE PASHA

Khereddine was born in the Caucasus Mountains and, as a *mamluk* recruit, was sent to Istanbul for training. He came to Tunisia as a soldier, quickly rose through the ranks, and entered the bey's administration. He became a noted reformer, famed for his *Aqwam-al-masalik* ("The Surest Path"), a blueprint for political and social reform in Muslim societies. He founded Tunis's celebrated Sidiqi College, which became a training ground for Tunisia's future leaders, including Habib Bourguiba, Tunisia's first president. It is an irony of history that a Circassian *mamluk*—most likely Christian by birth—is regarded as the father of the modern Tunisian state.

After his removal from office, Khereddine was summoned by the Sublime Porte to be grand vizier to Sultan Abdul Hamid.

The French Protectorate, 1881–1956

At the Congress of Berlin in 1878, Britain agreed to allow France a "free hand" in Tunisia in exchange for France agreeing to Britain's occupation of Cyprus. So it was no surprise when, in 1881, the French sent 30,000 troops into

Tunisia on the pretext of countering border raids by nomadic tribesmen into French-occupied Algeria. They headed straight for Tunis.

The French Consul Roustan rode up to the Bardo Palace, followed by General Bréart and his suite, armed with swords and revolvers. They were shown up to the first floor salon with its faded yellow damask. General Bréart wasted no time on compliments. He handed to the bey a draft ten-point treaty, written in French. The bey could not understand a word of it. He asked for a written Arabic translation, and was given the gist: a permanent French resident and French army would help maintain "the ancient relationship of friendship and good neighborliness" between the two countries. "At any rate you will grant me twenty-four hours for consideration?" asked the bey. "Certainly not. I expect an answer before eight o'clock tonight and shall remain here until I get one," Bréart replied. At about five o'clock the bey's courage failed. He put his signature to the document he could not read, writing his name in trembling Arabic characters.

Under the Treaty of Bardo, the bey remained Tunisia's titular head—though real authority passed to France's resident-general. The bey continued to appoint ministers of government— though real authority lay with a French resident attached to each ministry.

The next colonial building block was the Marsa Convention of 1883, by which France took responsibility for the Tunisian debt and disbanded the international financial commission. Foreign consuls surrendered their judicial authority over their nationals, a concession earlier wrested from the bey. The Convention also established parallel justice systems, under which Europeans were judged under French law and Tunisians under a modified form of Islamic law.

The French went about the business of land acquisition more discreetly than they did in neighboring Algeria. In Tunisia, they managed to get their hands on the best fertile land without confiscating property or displacing people, both of which had occurred in Algeria. Rather, they took over large tracts of the Cap Bon Peninsula and the Medjerda Valley, previously controlled by the bey or used by nomads for grazing. The citrus groves of Cap Bon are a legacy of this time, as are most of the country's wine-producing vineyards.

The south was too arid for agriculture and was largely ignored until the beginning of the twentieth century, when phosphate was discovered in the hills west of Gafsa. The massive mining operation begun by the French remains an important export earner for the Tunisian economy.

Europeans in Tunisia numbered about 100,000 in 1900, with Italians being the largest nationality group until the 1930s when the French gained that distinction. The French ruled in Tunisia with a much lighter touch than in Algeria, where the bey had been sent packing and the country incorporated into France. This led to some acquiescence from Tunisians, particularly from reformist disciples of Khereddine, who thought a limited dose of French rule might be therapeutic if it resulted in a modernization of Tunisia's institutions. This group, educated at Sadiqi College, became known as the "Young Tunisians"—akin to the "Young Turks" who were busy revitalizing the Ottoman Empire. Their major weapon was *Le Tunisien*, a French-language newspaper founded in 1907, which became the voice of Tunisian reform.

After the First World War, the reformers created the Destour (Constitution) Party, named for the short-lived Constitution of 1861, which demanded a representative form of government in which Tunisians would have the same rights as Europeans. The French responded by arresting the Destour leader. Two years later the aged bey urged adoption of the Destour program, failing which he would abdicate. The resident-general ringed the bey's palace with troops, and the request was withdrawn.

The Struggle for Independence, 1934–56
In 1934 a dynamic young Sorbonne-educated lawyer, Habib Bourguiba, broke with the Destour Party and formed a new party with a more radical

agenda—the Neo-Destour, whose tactics included mass protests and civil disobedience. In 1938 serious disturbances led to his arrest, and the party was officially banned. At the outbreak of war in 1939, Bourguiba and other Neo-Destour leaders were

deported to France. However, when the Germans occupied France, Bourguiba was shipped off to Rome because the Nazis regarded Tunisia as within Italy's sphere of influence.

The North African Campaign, 1942–3

The North African Campaign reached its climax in Tunisia. In November 1942 Tunis fell to Axis troops, leading to Allied saturation bombing of Tunisian ports. The Battle of Kasserine Pass in February 1943 was the first major engagement between American and German forces. On May 7, 1943, British armor entered Tunis and American infantry took the port of Bizerte. Six days later, Axis resistance in Africa ended with the surrender of 275,000 German and Italian prisoners of war.

The Italians wooed Bourguiba, hoping he would back the Fascist cause. But Bourguiba foresaw an Allied victory and never wavered in his support of the Free French. He was confident that "once liberated from the Nazi yoke, France would not forget her true friends."

After the war Bourguiba painfully came to the realization that France would bestow no tangible rewards on Tunisia for its wartime forbearance, and renewed his public agitation, which once more landed him in prison.

SECOND WORLD WAR CEMETERIES
War dead from Great Britain and the countries of the Commonwealth are buried near where they fell in eight cemeteries maintained by the Commonwealth War Graves Commission. The largest of these is near Mejez el-Bab, thirty-five miles southwest of Tunis. American war dead are buried at the North Africa American Cemetery and Memorial in Carthage. French cemeteries are at Enfidha and Gammarth. The German military cemetery is at Borj Cedria.

Independence

In July 1954, just two months after the defeat of French forces by Ho Chi Minh at Dien Bien Phu in Vietnam, the French premier, Pierre Mendes-France, announced that France was ready to negotiate autonomy for Tunisia. In June 1955 an agreement was reached and Bourguiba, who had spent half of the previous two decades in detention, returned to Tunis to a hero's welcome.

On March 20, 1956, Tunisia was formally granted full independence, with Bourguiba as prime minister. Within a year, the last bey had been deposed, the country had been declared a republic, and Bourguiba became Tunisia's first president.

The Tunisian Flag

The flag has a red five-pointed star and crescent, in a white circle on a red field. It derives from the Ottoman flag, reflecting Ottoman suzerainty over Tunisia from the sixteenth through the nineteenth centuries. The flag dates from 1831 and did  not change during or after the colonial period. The crescent moon, which Arabs believe brings good luck, and the five-pointed star are ancient Islamic symbols.

President Habib Bourguiba, 1956–87

Bourguiba was quick to introduce sweeping legal and social changes to create a modern secular state much as Tunisian reformers had dreamed of for more than a century. One of his first acts was to push for legislation mandating complete equality of the sexes. This is the Personal Status Code of 1956, still viewed as groundbreaking legislation in the Arab world. The Code abolished polygamy and divorce by renunciation (a husband divorcing his wife by saying three times "I divorce you"), and introduced judicial divorce for both sexes. It also set a minimum marriage age of seventeen for girls, and gave them the right to refuse an arranged marriage. Women were given the right to vote and run for political office.

Another innovation was the priority given to the social sectors of education, health, jobs, and housing. Twenty-five percent of the government's budget was devoted to education and 6 percent to health care. In all, the government's commitment to social programs greatly exceeded that of other developing countries. As a result of Bourguiba's policies, primary education became a reality for both sexes, and an excellent public health system was put in place. Present-day Tunisia shows his legacy: life expectancy is now seventy-four years, as compared with fifty years at independence.

Bourguiba regarded Islam as a force that was holding the country back and therefore sought to deprive religious leaders of their grass-roots role

in shaping society, in part by closing religious schools and abolishing Sharia (Islamic law) courts. In addition, more than 60,000 hectares of land that had financed mosques and religious institutions were confiscated. Not surprisingly, clerics vehemently opposed the changes and for a time resistance flared, particularly in Kairouan.

Bourguiba is remembered not only for leading his country to independence from France but also for creating a strong secular Tunisian identity, advancing women's rights, adopting bold reforms, improving literacy, and raising Tunisia's standard of living. On the bronze door of Bourguiba's mausoleum in Monastir appear the words, "The Supreme Combatant, the Liberator of Women, the Builder of Modern Tunisia."

An Islamic opposition emerged in the 1970s whose support increased dramatically following the use of the military to crush a general strike in

January 1978. At the same time, international pressure was being exerted on Tunisia to adopt democratic reforms, particularly after Bourguiba was declared president for life in 1974. The first multiparty elections were held in 1981, under circumstances considered neither free nor fair.

Anxious to avoid the upheaval and violence being caused by Islamic militants in Egypt and Algeria, Bourguiba's government spent much of the 1980s conducting a harsh and effective crackdown against the Islamist opposition. In early 1984 the withdrawal of a bread subsidy sparked six days of rioting. Bourguiba perceived an Islamist hand behind the riots and sent in the army. More than seventy people died. To ease tensions, the bread subsidies were reinstated.

On November 7, 1987, Prime Minister Zine el-Abadine Ben Ali, afraid that executing several Islamists convicted of plotting to overthrow the government—as demanded by Bourguiba—would spark a popular uprising, seized power in a bloodless palace coup. A team of doctors declared the eighty-three-year-old president physically and mentally incapable of carrying out his duties.

Bourguiba died in 2000 at the age of ninety-six, having lived his last years in his place of birth, the central coastal town of Monastir.

President Zine el-Abadine Ben Ali (1987–   )
Born in 1936 into a family of modest means in the small central coast town of Hammam-Sousse, Ben Ali chose a military career, where his talents were recognized. He was sent to France to study at Saint-Cyr and the Artillery School of Chalons-

sur-Marne. After his return, he rose up through the ranks to become Tunisia's head of intelligence. After brief stints as interior minister and minister of state for internal affairs, he became prime minister, his springboard to the presidency.

When he came to power in 1987, he promised greater democratic openness and respect for human rights. The concept of president for life was abolished, presidential term limits were established, and greater opposition party participation in political life was agreed to. But the ruling Neo-Destour Party, renamed the Democratic Constitutional Rally (RCD), has continued to dominate the political scene. Ben Ali ran for reelection unopposed in 1989 and 1994. In the multiparty era, he won 99.44 percent of the vote in 1999, and 94.49 percent in 2004. In both elections he faced weak opponents. The RCD won all seats in the Chamber of Deputies in 1989, and won all of the directly elected seats in 1994, 1999, and 2004. However, because of constitutional changes granting greater representation to opposition parties, currently five opposition parties share 37 of the 189 seats in the Chamber of Deputies. A referendum held in May 2002 allowed Ben Ali to run for a fourth term in 2004 and for a fifth, presumably his last term (due to age limits on presidential candidates), in 2009.

Bourguiba's ambitious program to emancipate women has been continued and even intensified. Half of all university students today are female. Women account for 21 percent of civil servants, 35 percent of doctors, and 63 percent of pharmacists. Life expectancy for women exceeds that of men—a rarity in the Muslim world. The government has supported a remarkably successful family planning program that has reduced the population growth rate to just over 1 percent per annum, an important ingredient in Tunisia's economic and social stability.

In the early 1990s, after an alleged Islamist coup plot was discovered, many suspected fundamentalists were imprisoned or fled into exile. Ben Ali moved to assuage the public mood by going on a well-publicized pilgrimage to Mecca and ordering that the Ramadan fast be observed in public. He also released political  prisoners, abolished the State Security Court, and limited police powers of detention.

Tunisia has long been a voice for moderation and realism in the Middle East. President Bourguiba was the first Arab leader to call for the recognition of Israel, in a speech at Jericho (then in Jordan) in 1965. In 1993, Tunisia was the first Arab country to host an official Israeli delegation as part of the Middle East peace process. The Government of Tunisia operated an Interests Section in Israel from April 1996 until the outbreak of the second Intifada in 2000. Israeli citizens routinely travel to Tunisia on their Israeli passports.

For a decade, starting in 1979, Tunisia served as interim headquarters of the Arab League after it left Cairo to protest the 1978 peace treaty between Egypt and Israel. In 1982 Yasser Arafat and the Palestine Liberation Organization (PLO) came to Tunis after leaving Beirut. They stayed at Hammam Plage, near the capital, until they relocated to the West Bank and Gaza in 1994 under the terms of the Oslo Accords. (The PLO Political Department remains in Tunis.)

Despite the commitment to move toward a democratic system and improve human rights, there are restrictions on freedom of association and speech, citizens do not enjoy political freedom, and torture and abuse of political prisoners are widespread, according to US State Department reports. Foreign media, including foreign-based satellite television channels, criticize the Tunisian government for the lack of press freedom. Tunisia ranks number 148 out of 167 countries in the 2006 Reporters Without Borders list of World Press Freedom rankings.

Nonetheless, Tunisians are generally proud of their country's reputation for stability and economic success in a volatile and largely impoverished region. A glance west toward Algeria—still struggling with Islamist violence after fifteen years of civil strife in which at least 150,000 people have died—or east to Libya—led for four decades by the erratic Muammar Gaddafi—convinces many Tunisians that Ben Ali's antidemocratic tendency is not of major concern.

> **The world is with the strong of the moment.**
> *Tunisian proverb*

GOVERNMENT

Tunisia has the attributes of a democratic government: a constitution, three separate branches of government, a multiparty system, and, most recently, multicandidate elections. But, in reality, effective power lies with the executive branch.

According to the Constitution of 1959, Tunisia is an independent and sovereign republic whose religion is Islam and whose official language is Arabic. The Constitution is based upon the principle of the sovereignty of the people and the separation of powers. As with other North African states, the Constitution proclaims Tunisia's identification with the Maghreb and the ideal of Maghrebi unity.

Executive power is in the hands of the president of the republic, who is head of state, and the prime minister, who is head of government.

The Constitution guarantees to the citizens of Tunisia basic liberties such as equality before the law and presumption of innocence in legal proceedings; freedom of expression, the press, association, and assembly; inviolability of the home; the right of public worship; and the right to travel within and outside the country. However, these liberties may be curtailed by law when necessary in the national interest.

The strength of the formal institutions of government has not been tested in a major way since they were put in place fifty years ago. Many critics have called for clearer, more effective distinctions between executive, legislative, and judicial powers.

Executive

The president is elected by universal suffrage for a five-year term. He appoints the prime minister and

council of ministers who exercise executive power under his leadership. He serves as commander-in-chief of the armed forces.

In 2002 the Constitution was amended to remove the three-term limit on any individual serving as president.

The Legislature

Legislative power is exercised by a National Assembly, consisting of the Majlis Al-Nuwaab (Chamber of Deputies) elected for five years and the upper house Majlis Al-Mustachareen (Chamber of Councilors) added by constitutional amendment in 2002. Of the 189 seats in the Chamber of Deputies, 152 seats are elected by popular vote and an additional 37 seats are distributed to opposition parties on a proportional basis as provided for in 1999 constitutional amendments. The first elections for the Chamber of Councilors were held in 2005.

The president may issue decree-laws when the chamber is not in session provided that they are submitted for ratification when the chamber reconvenes.

The Judiciary
The judicial system consists of a Supreme Court, ten Courts of Appeal, twenty-four Courts of First Instance, and eighty-three cantonal tribunals. Judges are appointed by the *Conseil superiore de la magistrature*, which is chaired by the president. No fewer than 24.5 percent of judges must be women. The judiciary is nominally independent, but responds to executive direction, especially in politically sensitive cases.

The courts have no jurisdiction over disputes between the executive and the legislature. The courts receive funding from and are administered by the Ministry of Justice.

Administration
The country is divided administratively into twenty-four governorates. The president appoints all governors.

THE ECONOMY
Despite high unemployment, Tunisia ranks among the most successful of developing country economies. Significant infrastructure investments have eased rural poverty and brought running water and electricity to even the most remote villages. Overall, the economy is growing steadily, helping to cement Tunisia's reputation as a relatively prosperous, stable, and modern nation. This growth, combined with continued high levels of funding for social programs, has led to a steady drop in the nation's poverty rate, from 40 percent in 1970 to 10 percent in 2000 and 6 percent today.

Eighty percent of Tunisians own their own homes. Two-thirds of Tunisians are middle-class.

In the 1960s Tunisia flirted with socialism, and moved to a mixed economy in the 1970s. Rigid state controls have now been dismantled and the economy liberalized. Commercial banks are free to participate in the foreign exchange market, and total convertibility of the Tunisian dinar is a near-term objective.

The government pursues prudent economic policies, though it still retains control over certain "strategic" sectors of the economy (finance,

hydrocarbons, aviation, electricity and gas distribution, and water resources). But the private sector is playing an increasingly important role. Tunisia is a founding member of the World Trade Organization (WTO) and is publicly committed to a free-trade regime and export-led growth.

Economically and commercially, Tunisia is very closely linked to Europe. Tunisia signed an Association Agreement with the European Union (EU), which went into effect on January 1, 2008. The agreement eliminates customs tariffs and other trade barriers on a wide range of goods and services. More than 75 percent of Tunisia's trade is with the EU—mainly France and Germany. EU member states also provide the bulk of foreign direct investment, much of which has come in under the government's privatization program launched in 1987. As of May 2006, the program had raised $1.9 billion, of which $1.4 billion was foreign capital. Many international companies have set up shop in Tunisia, attracted by its modern infrastructure, reasonable cost of living, convenient location, high literacy rate, and competent workforce. Tunisia is ranked as the most competitive economy of Africa in the 2007 edition of the *Global Competitiveness Report* issued by the World Economic Forum.

Tunisia's infrastructure includes six commercial seaports and six international airports. The contract to build a seventh international airport at Enfidha was awarded in March 2007. A tender for a deepwater port in the same region is expected also.

In 2007 GDP growth reached 6 percent. Despite the government's success in curbing the population growth rate, a demographic peak is now hitting higher education and the job market. Tunisia has invested heavily in education and the number of students enrolled at university has soared from 41,000 in 1986 to more than 360,000. Providing jobs for these highly educated people represents a major challenge for the government. Unemployment officially stands at 14.2 percent, but spikes even higher in some parts of the country.

Agriculture

Seventeen percent of Tunisia is arable land where wheat, wine grapes, tomatoes, potatoes, and peppers are produced, and another 13 percent is used for permanent crops (huge olive and citrus groves). About 25 percent of the labor force works in agriculture, which accounts for roughly 15 percent of GDP.

Tunisia's wines come from its northern vineyards. Important regions are Nabeul, Cap Bon, Bizerte, Ben Arous, and Zaghouan. The French and Italians planted the first industrial vineyards in the nineteenth century. The total wine production is about 24,000 tons a year.

The fertile areas of the country are the north and the central coast. In the southern desert and plateau, desert farming is precarious, but barley and dates are produced in quantity. The early growing season allows Tunisia to export fresh produce—such as tomatoes, lettuces, melons, citrus fruits, grapes, and more—to Europe before local crops ripen. Other popular agricultural exports include dates, figs, and almonds.

Much of the country's most recent agricultural investment has focused on irrigation schemes, well and dam construction, and programs to prevent soil erosion and desertification.

Manufacturing

Manufacturing and mining of phosphates and other minerals are major foreign exchange earners, accounting for more than 30 percent of GDP. Industries include petroleum, chemicals, automotive, textiles, leather, footwear, agribusiness, fishing, and electrical and mechanical manufactures. Sixty automotive assembly plants now operate in Tunisia. Handicrafts include carpets, pottery, and copper and leather goods for both local and export markets. A growing trend is European clothing firms subcontracting assembly work to Tunisian factories to produce for export.

The lumber sector draws on the oak forests of the northwest. Esparto grass, used commercially in the manufacture of paper and baskets, is cultivated in the central plateau.

Agribusiness includes flour milling; fish, fruit, and vegetable canning; olive oil processing; and sugar refining. The fishing industry, centered on Sfax, also contributes to the country's exports of sardines, mackerel, and cuttlefish.

Tourism and Remittances

Tourism is a major source of foreign exchange, representing about 20 percent of hard currency receipts, as well as an important sector for employment. In addition, the one million Tunisians living abroad make a significant contribution to the economy. Over the past five years, remittances from abroad averaged roughly 5 percent of Tunisia's GDP and 25 percent of its foreign currency earnings.

In 2006, more than six million (mainly European) tourists visited Tunisia, which has gained a reputation as one of the best-value destinations in the Mediterranean. Besides the resort towns of Hammamet, Port El Kantaoui, Sousse, and Monastir, visitors are attracted by the country's historic and cultural sites, Tunis and its attractions, the Sahara oases, and the *Star Wars* sites. A different clientele are the many North Africans who visit Tunisia for vacations and family reunions because their own countries are too dangerous (Algeria) or too straitlaced (Libya).

Tunisia is also making inroads as a medical tourism hub. Attracted by the country's excellent medical infrastructure and significantly lower costs, Europeans have plastic surgery and other medical procedures carried out in Tunisia. A typical tourist spends between 300 and 400 euros during his stay, while a medical tourist spends at least 2,500 to 4,000 euros—a clear boon to the Tunisian economy.

RELATIONS WITH THE WEST

Independent Tunisia got off to a rocky start with France. In 1961 Bourguiba demanded that France evacuate its military enclave at Bizerte, the last part of Tunisia still under French control. When France delayed, Tunisian troops invaded the base. French paratroopers flown in from Algeria launched a bloody retaliatory operation in which more than a thousand Tunisians died during ninety hours of fierce fighting. The French finally withdrew from Bizerte in 1963. French aid was suspended in 1964 after the abrupt nationalization by Tunisia of foreign-owned landholdings.

Bourguiba felt strongly, however, that Tunisia's future lay with the West, especially France and the United States. By the 1970s Tunisia's relations with France had been repaired. In the 1980s French human rights groups and the French government led a campaign demanding greater respect for human rights in Tunisia, but after bombings by Algerian Islamists in France starting in the mid-1990s, this pressure has eased considerably.

Tunisia opposed the US-led alliance in the 1991 Gulf War and was even less enthusiastic about the US-led overthrow of Saddam Hussein in 2003. Although the Tunisian "street" opposes the occupation of Iraq, relations between Washington and Tunis are good.

For a time after 9/11, Washington was fixated on the need to develop democratic institutions in the Muslim world. This led to increased pressure on Tunisia to allow multiparty free and fair elections. But Hamas' landslide victory at the polls in Gaza in 2006 and Hezbollah's strong showing in Lebanon seem to have dimmed Washington's ardor for democracy in the Arab world. The reason: the US national interest may be better served by having a stable, friendly, moderate government in Tunisia than by insisting on free and fair elections that bring unfriendly forces to power. In a visit to Tunisia in 2006, then US Secretary of Defense Donald Rumsfeld lauded Tunisia for its role in the struggle against international terrorism.

To date, Tunisia has taken great strides in the socioeconomic area and only small steps toward democracy. This is likely to continue.

VALUES &
ATTITUDES

At the crossroads of the Islamic and European worlds, Tunisia prides itself on being more liberal, tolerant, and culturally advanced than its North African neighbors. Its capital, Tunis, has an air of sophistication and *joie de vivre* quite unmatched in any city between Casablanca and Cairo. Tunisians are eager to absorb new ideas and innovations from abroad, but without sacrificing their values, which are shaped by Islam and its Arab culture.

RESPECT, DIGNITY, AND STIGMA

Among the most important Tunisian values are the showing of respect, the preservation of dignity, and the avoidance of stigma.

Showing Respect

One shows respect by speaking respectfully and addressing a person by his or her correct title. Respect is owed to those on a higher social status. This may be based on individual reputation, family, fame, wealth, and political and religious leadership. Young people show respect for their elders by visiting them first on special holidays. Some people with a sense of their own status do not visit those they consider lower in rank.

The general title of respect for men is *Sidi*, sometimes shortened in speech to *Si*. It is roughly comparable to "Sir" or "Mr." You can address any man as *Sidi* if you don't know his name and want his attention. *Sidi* can also mean "Master," "Lord," or "Saint," depending on context. For example, an older conservative Tunisian woman would call her husband *Sidi* and not use his first name. She might even call an older brother *Sidi* if there is a large age difference between them.

For a woman, the general title of respect is *Lella*, which can be prefixed to a personal or family name, or used alone to get the attention of a woman whose name you don't know. One can also use the common French titles *Monsieur*, *Madame*, and *Mademoiselle*—or *Docteur*, *Professeur*, *Ministre*, or *Ambassadeur*, where appropriate.

> When someone comes to you and shows you respect, serve him your dinner and make his bed.
>
> *Tunisian proverb*

Preserving Dignity

The emphasis placed on preserving a person's dignity is linked to the goal of achieving social harmony. A person who loses face may feel insulted, and may not easily forgive or forget. This means that frankness and honesty are not always seen as positive attributes in cases where they threaten a harmonious relationship. It is better not to put a person on the spot or cause him embarrassment. For example, a request for a substantial favor would be made indirectly, or by a third party. Visitors who are used to directness must learn not to give a straight refusal, which would cause the person making the request to lose face. It is best to give an answer that causes no embarrassment to either party. If rejecting the request, it is advisable to put the blame on an outside cause, to avoid possible personal offense. In the same vein, the person making the request will try to leave the door open by not asking for an immediate answer. It is all about "face."

If you are declining an invitation, it is considered more polite to say, "I'll try to come," than to say "no," or "I can't come." When an Arab is asked for something, he feels a sense of obligation to try to oblige. If asked directions in the street, and he doesn't know the answer, he will often rather guess than say he can't help, even if it would have been more helpful if he had simply said, "I don't know."

On the other hand, the general helpfulness of Arabs, especially to foreigners, is the plus side of the same coin. Tunisians value hospitality, warmth, and generosity. People are more important than time or money.

Tunisians are religious and deal with problems by saying that they are the will of God. They use phrases such as "*Insha'allah*" (God willing) and "*Allah ghalib*" (God is stronger) to express hopes or future intentions. In such an environment, the spoken word has power.

People believe in the power of blessings and curses. "May God preserve him for you" is a popular blessing for a newborn. Curses are serious business, not to be confused with casual swearing. Difficult times are explained as *maktoub* (fate), an attitude that provides comfort and encourages perseverance. This acquiescence is not indifference, but rather a survival tactic.

That is not to say that Tunisians are docile. They will make great efforts to maintain someone else's dignity and their own. They must defend the honor of themselves and their loved ones, and if they feel insulted tempers flare. For example, if a man's wife has been harassed, he cannot ignore it, and may well get into a fistfight over the issue. He does what it takes to restore his honor or dignity.

Avoiding Stigma

Tunisians will do their utmost to avoid *hishma,* or shame, which is an important concept. *Hishma* is quite unlike the Western concept of guilt. Guilt is where *you* know that you have done wrong. *Hishma* is where *others* know it.

There are myriad ways in which a person may acquire the stigma of *hishma*. Generally, these fall into the category of behavior outside the social norms: sexual deviancy, anything forbidden by Islam, or anything that brings shame on one's family. The range of *hishma*-generating events is mind-boggling. It can even include a man taking a job beneath his social status, such as a professor doing manual labor or working unusual hours.

STATUS AND SOCIAL STRUCTURE

Although there is considerable upward mobility in Tunisia, huge social gaps exist between rich and poor, educated and illiterate, urban and rural. Class distinctions based on wealth are the most apparent, with enormous differences between the wealthy bourgeoisie living in the affluent suburbs of Tunis and the rural and urban poor.

French colonial rule introduced Western-style education and competitive civil service examinations. In time, these innovations altered Tunisian society by creating a new class of administrators and professionals who joined the old aristocratic families and large landowners as elites. Wealth in one generation led to improved education in the next.

Since independence in 1956, the process of Westernization has continued—you'll see a great many town dwellers with laptops and iPods and wearing designer clothes. Ranged against them are many who are less receptive to Westernization and more oriented toward the Arab world and Islam. In recent years conservative elements have become more assertive, opening up a conflict between Western-style modernizers and those favoring traditional Islamic society.

SOCIAL NETWORKS

Tunisians have a wide social network drawn from their hometown, family, old school friends, neighbors, and acquaintances. These contacts are used both in business and in day-to-day affairs. For example, when a Tunisian needs a plumber, he's unlikely to use a directory; he'll consult his network. Calling old friends for favors and pulling strings are the norm. Connections are also the key to getting a good job, or sometimes *any* job. The underprivileged classes generally lack a strong social network. As a result, they often approach figures of authority with a cautious attitude and a degree of sycophancy.

In Tunisia, the group is more significant than the individual, and the family is the most important social unit of them all. Being on your own is considered a sad state, and your social network, family, neighbors, and friends are there to protect you from that.

Much time must be spent building and sustaining one's social network. This involves a lot of social interaction. If someone is ill, family and friends must go to see them. Likewise, when someone returns from a trip, family and friends will visit them to welcome them back. Friends and relatives call on newlywed couples in their marital abode to congratulate them. A new mother must be visited with gifts for the baby soon after the birth. It is especially important to visit neighbors and family on religious holidays. This means that friends and family visit each other frequently and unannounced, even late in the evening. Visits can last several hours, and hospitality demands that food and drink be served.

ISLAM AS A WAY OF LIFE

Islam is the official religion of Tunisia, and 98 percent of Tunisians are Muslim. The Christian and Jewish populations are minuscule. It is extremely rare to find a Tunisian who is openly agnostic or atheist. It is, in fact, considered highly offensive for someone to say that they do not believe in God. So if you are an atheist or agnostic, it's best to keep it to yourself.

Islam, which means "submission" in Arabic, is not simply a religion— it is a way of life. It defines one's relationship with God and plays an important role in interpersonal relations and daily life, especially during family events such as births, circumcisions, weddings, and funerals.

Abraham (*Ibrahim*) is honored as the father of Muslims, and biblical prophets, including Jesus, are respected, but Mohammed is considered the last and greatest of the prophets. He was born in 570 CE into a trading family in the Arabian city of Mecca, in present-day Saudi Arabia. In 610, he began to receive revelations and messages from Allah that prompted him to launch a vigorous campaign against idolatry. This so antagonized influential families in Mecca that he was forced in 622 to flee to the northern oasis town of Medina, now the second-holiest city in Islam. This migration, or *Hejira*, marks the beginning of the Islamic calendar.

By the time of Mohammed's death in 632, not only Mecca but most of the Arabian Peninsula had been converted to Islam. Mecca became the symbolic center of the faith—the place to which all Muslims turn to in prayer.

In Tunisia Islam is visible, audible, and tangible. Framed verses of the Koran adorn the walls of shops and houses in every Tunisian hamlet. Practically every Tunisian is within earshot of the *muezzin*'s call to prayer, which resounds five times a day, and everywhere one sees the faithful thronging to the mosque for midday prayers on Friday, the holiest prayer day.

THE FIVE PILLARS OF ISLAM

A sincere Muslim observes the five pillars of Islam to the highest degree possible:

Shahada: To make the profession of faith: "There is no God but Allah, and Mohammed is His Prophet."

Salat: To pray five times a day, at dawn, noon, afternoon, sunset, and night. A Muslim goes to a mosque if it is convenient, but may pray in practically any clean, relatively secluded spot. He faces Mecca to pray, aided by the position of the sun and stars, or the location of the *mihrab*, or prayer niche, inside the mosque. Before praying, a Muslim washes his hands, arms, feet, head, and neck in running water, which is available for the faithful outside every mosque.

Zakat: To give alms to the poor. You will often see Tunisians giving something to beggars.

Sawm: To observe a strict fast, believed to be spiritually cleansing, during the the daylight hours of the month of Ramadan.

The Hajj: To aspire to make the pilgrimage to Mecca, at least once in one's lifetime.

Importance of the Koran

Islam's holy book, the Koran (*Qur'an*), meaning
"recitation," is considered by Muslims to be the
word of God as dictated to the Prophet
Mohammed by the Angel Jibril (Gabriel) during
the month of Ramadan. The Koran is composed of
114 chapters, each called a *sura*, divided into verses
called *ayat*. It addresses codes of behavior, society,
and law. The written records of the Prophet's life,
the *Hadith*, are the second-most important Islamic
source. The *ulema* (Islamic jurists and scholars)
are charged with interpreting the Koran and other
writings, including the *Hadith*.

All Muslims commit verses from the Koran to
memory, and references to God form part of their
regular speech.

ARABIC'S KUFIC SCRIPT

Using the angular script known as Kufic,
which was ideal for stone carving, early
calligraphers carved verses from the Koran
on the Minaret of the Great Mosque of Sfax
and the Mosque of the Three Doors at
Kairouan, two of Islam's great architectural
achievements.

Sunni and Shia

Two branches of Islam emerged as a result of a leadership struggle in the early days of the religion. The Prophet Mohammed had no sons, so on his death the spiritual and temporal leadership of the movement (the Caliphate) passed to his father-in-law. The next two caliphs were drawn from the Prophet's tribe, the Quraish. The fourth Caliph was Ali, Mohammed's son-in-law. But Ali met a sad end. He was assassinated in 661 by the Governor of Syria, Mu'awiyah, who then founded the Ummayad Caliphate (deriving its name from the Ummaya clan).

Hussein, Ali's son and the Prophet's grandson, raised the standard against the Ummayad dynasty. But he perished in the year 680 at the Battle of Karbala, in present-day Iraq.

The schism in Islam dates from this event. The Shiites support the claims of Ali's successors as the legitimate authority in the Islamic world. The Sunnis, for their part, maintain that the Caliph should be a member of the Quraish tribe, but not necessarily a literal descendant of the Prophet. Although there are no great theological differences between the two branches, the split persists. Shiites are in the minority in the Islamic world, except in Iran and Iraq.

The Muslims of Tunisia have been overwhelmingly Sunni ever since the eleventh century, when the Zirids renounced their allegiance to their Berber Shiite overlords (the Fatimids) and returned the country to Sunni orthodoxy. It is estimated that 95 percent of Tunisia's Sunni Muslims belong to the Malekite

School, which is somewhat less rigid in its Quranic interpretation than other schools.

ATTITUDES TO ISLAMIC EXTREMISM

Tunisia is not fertile ground for Islamic extremism. The overwhelming majority of Tunisians do not support violence against innocent civilians in the name of Islam, no matter how much the perpetrators seek to justify it by calling it *jihad* (which literally means "struggle," and can apply to many other situations in life besides political struggle). This was made abundantly clear after an Al-Qaeda-linked attack against the El-Ghriba Synagogue on the island of Jerba in April 2002. A suicide bomber blew himself up in front of the synagogue, killing twenty-one people, many of whom were German tourists who had just stopped for a quick look at the synagogue. Tunisians were outraged by the attack and almost universally denounced it.

ATTITUDES TO FOREIGNERS

Marhaba—a word you will hear repeatedly—means "welcome" in Arabic. Tunisians are polite, courteous to strangers, and generally helpful to new foreign residents or tourists.

Many Tunisians have traveled and lived abroad for education or work. Others form their view of foreigners through Hollywood films and foreign serials shown on Tunisian TV, and by meeting tourists. This, of course, gives an incomplete view of what life is like abroad, and of what foreigners are like.

Tunisians admire the West's accomplishments, but may view its lifestyle as decadent or uncaring. They are troubled that, in the West, children move out of their homes before getting married, and elderly parents can be sent to nursing homes. To them, this represents a lack of family values.

The Tunisian-on-the-street is horrified at the idea that Islam has been typecast as the enemy of Western democracy and finds much to criticize in the West's policies toward the Middle East.

With France, the former colonial power, there is a love/hate relationship. Tunisians are infatuated with France and French culture, though they may see racism in France's colonial past and present immigration policies.

This does not imply that Tunisians are averse to relationships with foreigners. A foreigner who shows respect for their culture is warmly embraced. Regardless of how Tunisians feel about your government, they will be quick to accept you as an individual.

Tunisians share a common language and faith with their neighbors in the Arab world, naturally creating a strong bond. They refer to other Arabs as their "brothers," but even brothers have disagreements. Many Tunisians disapprove of the illiberal way that women are treated in some Arab countries. Conservative Arab satellite broadcasts are blamed for spreading a rigid and distorted view of Islam and for popularizing fundamentalist-style practices not viewed as authentically Tunisian, such as the Islamic head covering. As to other Muslims generally, there is a feeling of kinship with them, regardless of nationality.

Attitudes toward sub-Saharan Africans are rather complex. Tunis has worked hard to develop good relations with African governments and for the past five years has served as interim headquarters of the African Development Bank after civil war forced the bank to leave Abidjan in Cote d'Ivoire. But in a country where black skin was once considered tantamount to being a slave (*wasif*), there is some residual racism, particularly directed to non-Muslims. Also Tunisians tend to associate black Africans with increased crime rates and scams, tropical disease, and taking work away from Tunisians.

Foreigners enjoy religious freedom, provided they don't impose their own religion on Muslims. Christians and Jews report few problems, and although Eastern religions are less well-known, faith is generally respected. If you have strong views about Islam, it's best to keep them to yourself.

WOMEN IN SOCIETY

There can be little doubt that because of Habib Bourguiba's authoritarian rule, he was able to adopt and enforce laws on women's emancipation that stretched the boundaries of Tunisian cultural acceptance. Family planning clinics sprang up throughout Tunisia, giving women real choice. With fewer children to raise, women enthusiastically entered the labor force.

Today many Tunisian women live a complicated societal double existence. On the one hand, they benefit from a liberal legal and socioeconomic environment that is better than almost anywhere else in the Islamic world. There are as many girls as boys in school, and young women make up more than 50 percent of university graduates. Female literacy rose from 24 percent in 1966 to 77 percent in 2004. Many women now occupy jobs in government, industry, and the private sector. In terms of health, infant mortality is only

26 per 1,000 births, compared with 139 in 1966. On the other hand, these advances have reduced rather than eliminated the gap between the status of women and men. Women endure a lot of stress trying to follow a career or enter public life in a male-dominated society. Some men resent the formal employment of women when unemployment of educated men remains high, and also scorn the idea of women in public life.

If women do work outside the home, they hurry home after work to avoid *hishma*—the stigma that they could acquire if they were seen returning late. For them, the public social domains, such as cafés, are just as off limits as for any other woman.

Bourguiba once called the *hijab* (the veil worn by Muslim women) an "odious rag," and banned it from schools as a first step in eliminating it altogether. Not wearing it became for Tunisian women an expression of their personal liberty;

but renewed traditionalism has led to a resurgence in its use. In October 2006 the government launched a public campaign against wearing the veil in schools and government offices, arguing that the head scarf is not rooted in Tunisia's traditions or required by Islam. Instead Islamic dress was being promoted by extremists who were exploiting religion for their political ambitions. "If today we accept the head scarf, tomorrow we'll accept that women's rights to work and vote and receive an education can be banned, and they'll be seen just as a tool for reproduction and housework," said Hedi Mhenni, Secretary General of the ruling RCD Party, in October 2006.

"*INSHA'ALLAH*"

Submission to God is omnipresent in daily speech. "*Insha'allah*" means "If God wills"—an expression that Tunisians inject into almost every sentence when speaking about their thoughts or intentions for the future. Not to say "*Insha'allah*" is seen as tempting fate because good fortune is God's mercy, and misfortune is God's will.

Therefore, if talking in the future tense, "*insha'allah*" must be used. A Tunisian will never say, "I'm going to Sousse tomorrow." He will say, "I'm going to Sousse tomorrow, *insha'allah*." The final decision is that of God. If someone forgets to say "*insha'allah*," someone else will say it as a reminder. If someone asks, "Are you going to Sousse tomorrow?" and the reply is "Yes," the other person will add the missing "*insha'allah*."

Insha'allah is in vogue as an easy and noncommittal answer to a question, that might mean, "yes," "probably," "probably not," and "no." This can be very confusing and frustrating for Western visitors.

TOLERANCE AND DISCRETION

Though socially conservative, Tunisians are generally quite tolerant of Western behavior. But there are limits. For example, Tunisian society has yet to come to terms with overt homosexuality, which remains illegal under Tunisian law. There is a homosexual community in Tunisia, but they usually reveal their sexuality only to close, liberal-minded friends.

Local "beach gigolos" looking to pick up foreign men may circulate in some of the more touristy areas, and some foreign men travel to Tunisia specifically to seek this out. Lesbianism, on the other hand, seems totally off-limits.

Regardless of your sexual orientation, discretion is the key. Displays of romantic, sexual affection between two men are likely to result in hostility and possible violence. Also displays of affection by heterosexual couples, such as kissing on the street, are not advised.

chapter three

CUSTOMS & TRADITIONS

NATIONAL HOLIDAYS

Tunisia has a number of national holidays during which banks, public offices, schools, and most shops are closed. Though there are often street celebrations, most of these holidays are not as important to the average Tunisian as the religious holidays. However, many people take the opportunity to visit their families, so public transportation can be packed. Unlike the religious holidays, these holidays fall on fixed dates each year because they are based on the Gregorian or solar calendar used by government and business.

RELIGIOUS HOLIDAYS

The Islamic calendar is based on the phases of the moon and consists of twelve lunar months, beginning with the *Hejira*, Prophet Mohammed's flight from Mecca to Medina in 622 CE (1 AH in the Islamic calendar). Since the lunar calendar has approximately 354 days, religious holidays occur eleven days earlier each solar year.

Islamic holidays depend upon a visual sighting of various phases of the moon, so published schedules of these holidays in date books and calendars are only approximations.

NATIONAL HOLIDAYS

New Year's Day (January 1): This day is celebrated as a secular holiday, which gives Tunisians a day to recover after New Year's Eve parties.

Independence Day (March 20): commemorates the day that Tunisia became independent from France in 1956.

Youth Day (March 21): honors and celebrates youth and youth workers.

Martyr's Day (April 9): commemorates the Tunisian martyrs who died in 1938 seeking independence from France.

Labor Day (May 1): May Day is celebrated in Tunisia as the internationally recognized day to honor labor.

Republic Day (July 25): commemorates the day when Tunisia became a republic with Habib Bourguiba as president in 1957.

Women's Day (August 13): marks the anniversary of the adoption of the Personal Status Code by the Tunisian Parliament on August 13, 1956.

Evacuation Day (October 15): commemorates the day in 1963 when the last of the French troops evacuated their military base at Bizerte.

New Era Day (November 7): commemorates the day in 1987 when Zine El Abadine Ben Ali assumed the presidency from Habib Bourguiba.

Islamic New Year
Hejira is celebrated on 1 Moharram, the first day of the first month of the Islamic calendar. There is no public celebration, though usually government and religious officials mark it with a special function.

Prophet Mohammed's Birthday

Moulid-an Nabi, or simply Moulid, celebrates the Prophet's birthday, and falls on the twelfth day of the third month of the Islamic year. Moulid is a great family celebration. Children are decked out in their best clothes and given special sweets.

Ramadan

Ramadan, the ninth month of the Muslim year, is especially holy because the word of God, as represented in the Qur'an, was revealed at this time to the Prophet Mohammed by the Angel Jibril (Gabriel). This is a time of fasting (*sawm*). Between sunrise and sunset Muslims abstain from eating, drinking, and smoking. Exemptions are made for children, pregnant women, the elderly, and the sick. Each day the fast ends at sundown. Immediately after prayer, one eats something light. Mohammed was said to break his fast with a few dates and a glass of milk, and many people like to keep up this tradition. Then the *iftar,* a huge meal, follows. Sometimes people eat more during Ramadan than normal, and gain weight! You might expect there to be little interest in food during a month of fasting, but the reverse is true. Women take great pride in preparing their best dishes for the *iftar*, and the magazines are full of recipe ideas.

Evenings are lively and festive, and feature special foods, carnivals, shopping, and street festivals. For the past twenty-five years, the Medina Festival has brought leading Arab musicians, artists, and intellectuals to enliven Ramadan nights in the former palaces and mansions of the Tunis Medina. Similar events are held at historic venues elsewhere in Tunisia.

In olden days there would be a procession to a site where the crescent moon could be clearly seen before the fast was proclaimed, with lanterns to light the way. This practice survives in elaborate decorations being hung outside homes, shops, and in the streets during Ramadan, and in children being given a colorful lantern.

Charity and goodwill are especially valued during Ramadan. A stranger will give a date or a fig to a person who has not been able to make it home in time for *iftar*. Outside mosques, *iftar* tables are laid out for those who are fasting and have nowhere to eat. These tables, known as *mawa'id al-rahman* ("tables of the merciful"), are set up for the needy and paid for by wealthy donors. Any one without an *iftar* to attend may line up to get a place, the idea being that no one should have to break his or her fast alone.

If you are invited to an *iftar*, be sure to show up on time! Otherwise, you may find Tunisians waiting for you, the honored foreign guest, and prolonging their fast. As the author can attest, this is very embarrassing!

While all-night parties are popular, most Muslims manage to snatch a little sleep before eating a predawn meal, known as the *suhur*, which has to keep them going for the whole day.

Foreigners, while not expected to fast themselves, should be respectful to those who do. It is *not* a good idea to eat or drink in the street while others are fasting. Some cafés and restaurants will be open, so you can eat and drink discreetly indoors during Ramadan.

Since it is a sacred month, Tunisians dress modestly during Ramadan, even those who normally wear flashy clothes. For the same reason, drinkers often give up alcohol for the month.

Keeping the fast is especially hard when Ramadan falls during the summer months, when days are longest and hottest. Usually the first few days are the worst when fasters are still adjusting to not eating, drinking, or smoking. Traffic jams increase and tempers flare as people rush home from work just before the *iftar* to join friends and families. Traffic accidents are endemic at that time. Don't even think of trying to get a taxi. Also, expect workmen and household help to slow down during Ramadan.

In 1960 and 1961, President Bourguiba encouraged Tunisians not to fast, arguing that Tunisia could not afford the decline in productivity that occurs during Ramadan. He cited the Koran, claiming that Tunisia was engaged in a *jihad* against underdevelopment and that Islam excused participants in a *jihad* from fasting. But popular resistance to his campaign against fasting was intense, and many religious leaders openly rejected Bourguiba's reinterpretation of Ramadan. In the end, Bourguiba had to back off. Since then, Ramadan has been observed traditionally.

Eid al Fitr
This three-day festival marks the end of the Ramadan fast. It is customary to have prayers at sunrise at the mosque, followed by a celebratory family meal. This is a time for exchanging gifts,

buying new clothes for the children, and traveling home to see loved ones.

Eid al Adha

This, the "Feast of the Sacrifice," marks the end of the Muslim pilgrimage to Mecca. A three-day holiday commemorates the story of the willingness of Abraham to obey God by sacrificing his son. In the Bible the son is Isaac; in Islam it is Ishmael. Later, Abraham is allowed to sacrifice a ram in his son's place. In remembrance of this, Muslims offer a sacrifice of their own by slaughtering a cow or ram and donating a portion of the meat to the sick or poor. This feast takes place on the tenth day of the last month of the Islamic year.

LOCAL AND REGIONAL FESTIVALS

From the smallest settlements to the largest, festivals are omnipresent throughout Tunisia. They are lively affairs and celebrate such diverse events, activities, or subjects as the arrival of spring, autumn harvests, sea sponge fishing, Arab horses, Tunisian music (*malouf*), and the lives of local "saints" (see below). Any foreigner who happens to pass through town during one of the numerous summer festivals will be welcomed and urged to join in. Before long you will find yourself dancing and sharing a cup of tea.

Some of the most interesting festivals are in the desert oases. Douz, the last major oasis town before entering the Sahara, hosts a festival that was originally a Bedouin marriage market.

It attracts an estimated 50,000 visitors a year to an event that includes a lively mix of traditional music, dance, camel and greyhound racing, storytelling, and feasting. Another is the Oasis

Festival held in Tozeur, a pleasant town bounded on one side by an enormous stand of palm trees and on the other by a desolate salt lake, the Chott el-Jerid.

SUPERSTITIONS

Certain folk beliefs and customs, most likely pre-Islamic in origin, persist in modern Tunisia, especially among the poor and uneducated. Sophisticated urbanites may denounce these practices as backward and un-Islamic, but they are strongly rooted in the Tunisian psyche.

A *djinn*—from which the English word genie derives—is a spiritual being that may play a role in human affairs if called upon. Belief in *djinns* is widespread in the Muslim world. One protects against *djinns* by wearing an amulet of verses from the Koran.

Another common superstition is fear of the Evil Eye: an envious person can cause your good luck to disappear by casting the Evil Eye on you.

> ## How could the Evil Eye hit you, the bowlegged one!
>
> *Tunisian proverb*
> (A person with physical defects need not fear the Evil Eye because no one envies him.)

To avoid the Evil Eye, Tunisians are quite discreet about discussing good things. They may not talk about the health and beauty of a child or reveal a new job until they actually begin work.

One guards against the Evil Eye by reciting verses from the Koran and wearing the *Khomsa,* or Hand of Fatima (daughter of the Prophet). Hands of Fatima are hung above doorways and dangle from car mirrors throughout Tunisia. Silver and gold earrings and pendants of Hand of Fatima design are among the most popular jewelry in Tunisia.

Precious stones having magical powers (*khatems*) are the special province of Tunisian witches. Among the most potent of these are the bloodstone, which cures toothaches, the topaz, which counteracts jaundice, and the diamond, which cures all diseases. The turquoise cures eye disease and assures an abundance of milk in nursing mothers.

President Bourguiba unsuccessfully tried to root out these beliefs. He once devoted part of an important speech to criticizing belief in the Evil Eye, the avoidance of the numbers ten and fifteen, and the custom of blessing a new house by putting vessels of food in all the rooms to placate the *djinns* of the place. He urged Tunisians to discard these outmoded ideas, which he said were unworthy of Islam.

VISITS TO LOCAL SHRINES

In each town or community in Tunisia there will probably be a tomb of a holy man or "saint," which attracts the faithful in large numbers. These shrines are probably a continuation of a pre-Islamic nature cult and may reflect unusual features in the landscape, such as caves, hilltops, springs, or odd-shaped trees. Such a shrine may be the object of an annual festival that draws together people from a particular community, such as a village, extended family, or tribe, to honor the holy man in a vibrant event, bursting with color and festivity. Women play a greater role in these ceremonies than in formal Islam, which is heavily male-centered.

People visit a shrine for many reasons, such as to request help from the shrine's "saint" or to

thank him for favors granted. This visit may turn into an annual ritual of reconnection between the individual or his family and the holy man. People fear that if they do not seek this reconnection, the "saint" will feel slighted and send his *djinns* to afflict them. This is a popular folk explanation for illness or misfortune.

Properly, only God can grant favors, because sanctification of a person through sainthood is not permissible under Islam. But the role of a holy man serving as an intermediary to help a person connect with God is well established in popular culture.

These beliefs are linked to Sufism, the inner or mystical dimension of Islam that originated in the eighth century. There are many Sufi orders in Tunisia that gather at the mosque or tomb of their "saint" or holy man and follow a particular *tariq* (path), or way of worshipping, more attuned to a mystical communion with God than a literal studying of the Koran. Once, Sufi orders had great prestige in Tunisia, with close ties to the court of the bey, but as Tunisia moved toward independence, they supported the powers-that-be and their reputation suffered. Today Sufis are a small minority.

chapter four

MAKING FRIENDS

Most Tunisians have a circle of friends who play an important part in their lives. Many friendships are formed at an early age, in one's hometown, at school, or at college, and last a lifetime. Tunisians are relatively egalitarian in their interpersonal relations, and the circle is large. They put a lot of time and effort into their friendships, from which they expect trust and commitment. Maintaining a friendship is no less intensive, but people expect to see their friends often, and to be intimately concerned with their lives.

Boys are allowed to socialize in groups outside the home; but society imposes stricter rules for girls. In the rural and poorer classes particularly, girls, when they are allowed out of the home, are under strict parental control. Male–female friendships are not common, except in the more permissive urban environments.

Foreigners are on the receiving end of much warmth and hospitality, so it is relatively easy for them to meet Tunisians. Meet one Tunisian, and before long you are introduced to many in his extended social network. But this should not be confused with real friendship, which is acquired only through repeated interaction over time.

GREETINGS

Greetings are important in Tunisia, and should not be neglected. Tunisians will base their opinion of someone on the way they greet them. Expressions of warmth and concern are integral to the ritual of greeting, and it is normal to inquire about the other person's health and family before moving on to other topics of conversation.

People of the same sex greet each other with affection. Women kiss on both cheeks, and may respectfully kiss the hand of an elderly relative. Men who know each other well also kiss each other on both cheeks. A pat on the back is an extra sign of warmth. Handshakes between men need to be strong and firm, as limp handshakes are considered insincere. It is also quite common to see men *or* women—not the two together—walking hand-in-hand; it is no indication of sexual orientation. After a handshake, many rural people also kiss their right hand, then lay it flat on their heart to signify warmth and sincerity.

The rules are different when greeting the opposite sex; minimal physical contact is the norm. A man should not extend his hand to a woman he does not know well—he should wait for her to extend her hand first. If she does not, he should simply bow his head in acknowledgment. Public displays of affection are unacceptable, even between husband and wife.

It is considered rude to see an acquaintance and not greet him, even if he seems busy or is engaged in conversation with someone else. A distant wave is not sufficient. When entering a shop or office, a person greets the owner or staff.

When Tunisians meet, the conversation goes something like this: "*Salaam Aleikom*" (May peace be upon you). "*Aleikom El Salaam*" (And peace be upon you). "*Labas? Labas Alik?*" (How are things? [*Labas* literally means "no harm;" *labas alik* asks about your personal well-being.]) "*Labas, alhamdulillah*" (No harm, thanks be to God). "*Bekhair?*" (Are you well?) "*Bekhair*" (Fine).

The standard morning greeting is "*Sabah El-Kheer*" (literally, Morning of Joy). One can give the same reply or say, more warmly, "*Sabah El-Noor*" (Morning of Light).

Other useful greetings are "*Ass'lama*" (Hello), "*Tass'bah ala Kheer*" (Good night), and "*Bisslama*" (Good-bye). To thank someone, you can say "*Merci Alayk,*" "*Inshallah Merci,*" "*Barakallaw Fik,*" or the more formal "*Shokran.*"

If you learn a few phrases of Arabic, and use them, your efforts will be truly appreciated.

MAKING CONVERSATION

Tunisians like small talk and gossip, so if you want to get on well with them it makes sense to cultivate the art of conversation. Speak clearly and plainly in order to avoid misunderstandings.

Don't try to dominate the conversation, but allow them to hold forth. Listen respectfully to their comments, and avoid arguments. A good listener is often a better conversationalist than a prolific talker.

Taboo Topics
There are several topics of conversation that are
best avoided, including Tunisian and Middle
Eastern politics. Be careful if you criticize the
regime, because officials, waiters, and taxi drivers
may understand more English than you think.

Another sensitive subject is Islam. You should
steer away from debates about the respective
merits of Islam and other religions. There is
plenty of room for misunderstanding in matters
theological. You may feel awkward, especially if
someone tries to convert you or expresses
opinions about your own religion that you know
to be incorrect. The best way to resist an effort to
convert you is to say that you're pleased with your
religion. Tunisians respect a person of faith and
will accept your decision.

Jokes are best avoided. It is not that Tunisians
lack a sense of humor, but humor, unless it is very
straightforward, does not travel very well.

Recommended Topics

Tunisians enjoy talking about their families, and especially the achievements of their children. A male visitor, however, should be careful not to show too great an interest in the female members of the household. In traditional households it is best not to mention them at all.

There are plenty of other topics that can be freely discussed. Sports, especially soccer, are popular among men. Television, films, music, and food are good, neutral topics, and there is always that perennial standby, the weather.

Tunisians like to hear about your experiences in their country, and you should be as complimentary as possible. They are very proud of their country and its achievements, particularly in relation to its neighbors, and appreciate having their views confirmed. Many are curious to learn about your country and where you live and what you do. Also you may be asked about educational institutions in your country.

HOSPITALITY

Tunisians, and Arabs generally, are masters of hospitality, and if you visit them at home you will almost certainly be served something to eat and drink. If they think you will be dining alone, they may insist on inviting you home for dinner.

If you are dining out with a Tunisian who insists on paying the bill, you should also insist on paying. There will probably be a push and a pull, and the more determined person will finally pay. If your dining companion pays for the meal, you should return the invitation on a later occasion.

As in many Arab cultures, in Tunisia the guest is revered. Particularly if they are foreign guests, Tunisians feel responsible for their well-being. They are genuinely concerned about the visitor's comfort and satisfaction with his trip.

INVITATIONS HOME

If you are invited to a Tunisian's home, it is polite to accept. Check to see if your spouse is included in the invitation. Conservative Tunisians may not entertain mixed-sex groups. In fact, you may never meet the host's wife!

Dress well, and pay close attention to details, such as polished shoes. This shows respect toward your hosts. It is best to err on the side of formality.

Take a gift of pastries, nuts, fruit, cake, candy, or flowers. Don't take alcohol, unless you know your host well, and that he drinks. Gifts are not opened when received, so don't be offended if your gift is put aside without comment.

When you arrive, offer to remove your shoes at the door. First-time visitors may be given a tour of the home, especially if there have been renovations or new furniture. On such an occasion guests might congratulate the hosts with "*Mabrouk*," a wish also used for weddings, graduations, or new employment. It is polite to give compliments on the home.

It's increasingly common in urban Tunisia to sit around a table on chairs and eat from separate plates with utensils. But traditionally, people sit

TABLE MANNERS

- Do not begin eating until the host blesses the food or begins to eat.

- When eating, Tunisians use their right hand to take food from a common bowl. Use bread as a scoop, and help yourself from the part of the bowl that is in front of you— don't reach over to take something from the other side.

- As an honored guest, choice morsels will be put in front of you. You can use either hand when eating from your own plate, and you may be given a spoon to eat couscous.

- If you finish what's on your plate, you will be served again because your act of clearing the plate suggests you are still hungry.

- A host will often insist that guests have second or third helpings, and it is polite to accept. It is considered good manners to try a little of everything.

- When a person has eaten enough, he expresses satisfaction with the meal by saying, "*Khamsa ou khmis aalik*" (You have done an excellent job), or "*Hamdullah*" (Thanks to God).

- Burping after a meal is considered rude.

on the floor around a low, round, wooden table (*mida*). The guest of honor usually sits next to the host. In traditional homes, women may not be present, or may eat in a separate room.

A hand-washing basin will be brought to the table before the meal is served. Hold your hands over the basin while water is poured over them, and dry them on the towel provided. The basin will be brought around the table again at the end of the meal.

Expect lots of food. Tunisian women usually go out of their way to put on a big spread for a guest, and even in a modest home the meal will not be modest. Meals are not served in courses. All the food is placed together in the middle of the table.

It is impolite to leave immediately after the meal. Instead, the host will lead the guests to the sitting area to have tea or coffee with dessert. After these have been finished, you can gently start your good-byes. At the end of the evening, the Tunisian host will politely walk with his visitors to the door, and will not shut the front door until the guests are out of sight.

chapter five

PRIVATE &
FAMILY LIFE

A fundamental split—between public and private—divides all of Tunisian life. Private life occurs only within the domain of the home, which creates and respects privacy. The public

domain is any interaction outside of the home. This division of public and private is reflected in traditional architecture. The high, protecting walls of the *dar araby*, the traditional Arab house, separate inside from outside, private from public. There is no front porch, manicured lawns, backyard, or anything else visible from the outside. There is a lovely private courtyard, maybe even a garden, but well hidden from public view. Even the interior architecture defends privacy. There are no halls, no connecting rooms; each room is a mini-dwelling with one door opening on to the central courtyard. Therefore: no surprise visitors.

Women traditionally lead cloistered lives shielded from public view by the walls of the *dar araby*. Laundry, cooking preparations, and myriad household chores command the central courtyard. This is the women's domain.

THE HOUSEHOLD

The family is the center of social life, and the typical household is family based. It usually consists of the nuclear family; it can include the extended family, but rarely nonrelatives. Children move out of the parental home only to move into a new marital home, and elderly parents move in with their children when they can no longer look after themselves. It is uncommon for people to live alone.

From a Tunisian Web Site

"There are so many rules and customs in my culture that we have to be extra careful over the smallest things for fear of offending somebody. The father of my brother's friend got really mad at his son one day because they walked into the house from the kitchen door and not the front door. What made the father even angrier was the fact that he was eating cactus fruit when the kids came into the house. To him it was humiliating, first that a guest entered thru the kitchen door and second that they saw him eating cactus fruit [see page 121]. The mother gave the son a long speech about manners and how he dared to bring a guest into the house thru the kitchen door, and how it humiliated the father."

In a traditional household, family roles are clearly defined. The father is boss, breadwinner, and decision maker, and his rulings are rarely questioned. The wife is expected to take care of the domestic duties of shopping, cleaning, cooking, and looking after the children, even if she has an outside job. Tunisian women tend to be very house-proud.

The eldest son takes over family responsibilities when the father reaches retirement age or is incapable of continuing. Traditionally, younger members of the family defer to older members, and women to men. Middle- and upper-class urban women may be free of this structure, sharing the decision-making power and daily chores with their husbands.

> "The girl from Tunis has the word ready in her mouth. The girl from Nabeul must wait until she consults with her mother."
>
> *Tunisian proverb*

About 80 percent of Tunisian families own their own homes. A typical home is painted white and trimmed with blue. It has formal and family living rooms, three bedrooms, a large kitchen, and a veranda. The floors are almost always tiled, and kitchens and bathrooms have elaborate tiling on the walls. Wood is scarcely used, and is limited to doors and window frames. The best furnishings are kept for the formal living room, which probably includes a sofa and china cabinet.

Access to electricity and plumbing is standard in urban areas, and is generally available in the rural areas.

Urban Life

There are two distinct styles of urban housing: *medina* houses and *ville nouvelle* apartments or villas.

Interlaced by a network of narrow walkways and passages, the older neighborhoods in and around a historic *medina* contain magnificent examples of traditional Islamic urban architecture. Behind a large, nondescript door there may be a sumptuous palace—or something akin to a hovel. The typical *medina* home has interestingly asymmetrical rooms on one or two floors, and squat toilets, although there have been some imaginative and attractive alterations made in recent years.

The three main sites for public interaction in the *medina* are the mosque, the market, and the public bath. They link Friday prayers with urbanity. The market (essentially a municipal farmers' market) attracts people for trade and exchange, and the public bath reflects the concern with personal cleanliness from a time when houses did not have their own bathrooms.

The *ville nouvelle* is an entirely different city, with its tall, shuttered windows, wrought-iron balconies, and cafés and patisseries. A typical

apartment is quite large, with several rooms for use as sitting rooms or bedrooms. There may or may not be built-in closets (not traditional in Tunisian homes) but there are likely to be a

Western toilet and a regular bathtub and shower.

Rural Life

Some rural people live in villages, and others live in scattered homesteads near their fields. People often leave some distance between themselves and their neighbors, seeking privacy. Depending on the status and wealth of the family, a rural home could have just one or two rooms or be much larger, with a protected courtyard. Formerly, Tunisia had a substantial nomadic population living in tents. Given Tunisia's water scarcity problems, rural people may have to carry water from a distant well, spring, or standpipe.

In rural areas, the weekly *souq* (market) is a center of activity. People come to buy goods and produce, to trade, and to socialize.

DRESS

There is not one statement about dress in Tunisia that would uniformly apply to all Tunisians. Clothing varies according to class, personal taste, and specific demand. Most people probably wear both modern and traditional clothes, for different occasions, and own some of each. Casual European or American-style clothes, varying enormously in quality, are the norm among the younger crowd. Most urban women dress in Western clothes and do not veil themselves. Upper-class women are extremely fashion conscious, with France and Italy being the fashion templates. Shorts and bathing suits are never worn in public, except in resort areas.

The traditional *fouta*—a brightly colored piece of cloth that becomes a dress when clasped together with silver jewelry or pins—is still worn in the countryside. Many town or city women wear the enveloping, white, sheetlike affair known as the *safsari*.

Countrywomen wear their hair up and covered, letting it down for celebrations and special occasions. A revival of religious and social conservatism in the 1990s has led to greater use of the Islamic head scarf or *hijab*.

Through the Eyes of a Western Woman

"At first encounter you may find the *safsari* abhorrent—obviously a male-inspired instrument of oppression. However, after two years of careful and deliberative dressing for public view, I recognize the benefits. One, it's clean, it protects against dust on the street and dirt in public transportation. Two, it's easy. You can throw it on like a bathrobe—never mind what's under it— and run to do an errand on a split second's notice, and be perfectly proper on the street. And three, it guards from prying eyes, prevents insults, and insures safety and well-being."

(Peace Corps Notes)

Traditional dress for Tunisian men includes baggy pants and a long robe, or *jalabiyya*, and a *chechia*, the distinctive red or brown felt hat, either rounded or flat on the top, of Andalusian origin.

GROWING UP IN TUNISIA

Children are considered a blessing from God and have a special place in Tunisian society. They are loved and pampered. Tunisian mothers, like Arab mothers generally, are doting and indulgent. Children stay up late and are often taken out. Babysitters are rarely needed, family members being usually available for the odd occasion.

It is normal for strangers to be affectionate and tactile with children. Don't be surprised if your child is whisked away by a cooing waitress at a restaurant or offered sweets by a stranger. Even macho teenage boys will fuss over a baby.

Primary and Secondary Education

Education is highly valued in Tunisia. It is free and compulsory for both sexes until the age of sixteen. In the classroom, boys and girls sit together, and are taught in French and Arabic. For the past decade, English study has been part of the curriculum.

> An old person will act according to his habits, and a young person according to his education.
>
> *Tunisian proverb*

The number of children in primary school (*école de base*) rose fivefold in the first twenty years of independence. Today practically every boy and girl in the country between the ages of six and eleven attends the six years (Grades 1-6) of *école de base*. Then come three years (Grades 7-9) of middle school (*collège*), followed by four years of *lycée* (Grades 10-13).

A British Mother's Opinion of Tunisian State Primary Schools

"Tunisian education is fast, furious, intensive and very strong. It doesn't matter that kids begin at six instead of four, as they soon catch up and end up miles ahead of their English counterparts. Language teaching is very good: Arabic at six, French at eight, and English from age ten. In as little as two years, the French is practically at O Level standard and beyond!

"Facilities are very basic. The primary schools do not have large sports fields or gyms. Toilets are often the basic 'hole in the floor' type. Desks are arranged in rows facing the board, like 1950s Britain.

"Discipline is strong. The law is that teachers cannot hit the children, but they do. Only you can decide whether you think this is a plus or not, but it does seem to cure the ill behavior that British schoolkids suffer from. On the whole, the children are more polite (you do get the odd one!) and bullying is a lot less frequent than in Britain."

After completing middle school, a student can leave school provided he or she takes three additional years of specialized, nonacademic training in a field such as carpentry, automobile repair, hairdressing, home economics, or restaurant work. This leads to the granting of a *diplome technique*. Virtually every school graduate is computer literate.

Further and Higher Education
In the tenth grade, students choose one of two tracks: *Lettres* (humanities and social sciences), or *Sciences* (mathematics and science). At the end of the thirteenth grade students take the rigorous *Baccalauréat* exam, or "*bac*." As a general rule, one takes the *bac* in French for science, mathematics, and economics, and in Arabic for arts and literature.

From Magharebia Online, June 4, 2008
Today in Tunisia, 156,013 students face an
annual event eagerly anticipated and often
dreaded by students and parents alike: the
Baccalauréat exam. A typical Tunisian family starts
preparations weeks before the onset of the *bac*,
scheduled for June 4 this year. Families spare no
effort to offer their children a convenient
environment so they can study.

"This is a decisive time for my daughter
and for the entire family," Saida Saiem told
Magharebia. Saida, whose daughter, Nour, is
majoring in empirical sciences, said that in the
days before the exam, the whole family has
been "on the alert to offer Nour the optimum
ambience so she can succeed."

According to figures released by the Ministry
of Education and Training, 58 percent of
students taking the exam are girls. The number
of students taking the *bac* in 2008 increased by
nearly 9 percent, compared to 2007 figures.
Tunisian families are well aware that the *bac* is
the gateway to college for their sons and
daughters.

After a major reorganization of the state
university system in 1988, Tunisia now has seven
universities and twenty-two higher institutes of
technological studies and teacher training. In
addition, there is a growing number of private
universities and institutes. Distance learning is
provided by a virtual university located in Tunis.

NATIONAL SERVICE

Under the military conscription law first adopted in 1959, all physically able male citizens reaching the age of twenty are technically required to serve in the armed forces for one year. But the number of young men who reach draft age each year—currently more than 100,000—greatly exceed the military's requirements, so most young Tunisian males do not serve.

FAMILY OCCASIONS

Family occasions are colorful affairs. They are soaked in tradition and ritual, and require the attendance and support of all family members.

With every Muslim enjoined to make the pilgrimage to the holy places of Mecca and Medina, the departure of a family member on pilgrimage and his or her return are ritualized by visits to mosques, gifts, and celebrations. To reflect his or her new status, the returned pilgrim is addressed as "*Hajj*" or "*Hajja*" (pilgrim).

The main stages of life are ritualized in Islam—birth, naming, circumcision (for boys), marriage, illness, and death.

Birth

When a baby is born to a Muslim family, the call to prayer is whispered into the newborn's right ear, to bring the baby into an awareness of God from the first moment of life. A week later, at a gathering of family and friends, a sheep or goat is sacrificed and the child is formally named. Mothers often sew a small verse from the Koran into a pouch attached to her newborn's clothes to keep the "Evil Eye" away and protect the infant from harm.

When the baby is one year old, and able to sit up, an *El Qaada* (sitting ceremony) is usually held. The infant is placed on a miniature rocking chair and presented with gifts. It is also around this age that girls' ears are pierced.

Circumcision

Boys between the ages of one and six are circumcised. The boy is dressed in a traditional outfit called the *Kiswa Tounsia*, often in a white robe or suit, and an elegant *chechia* hat. A religiously trained circumciser performs the procedure in front of invited guests. Families often hire traditional musicians and invite relatives and friends for an evening of celebration.

Many urban Tunisian parents are now opting for circumcision by a medical professional in a hospital, with guests invited for a small celebration at home afterward. The event is more hygienic, and less distressing for many parents.

Marriage

In traditional families, parents search for prospective sons- and daughters-in-law when their children reach marriageable age. Tunisian men often delay marriage, as a man is expected to provide a considerable dowry to his bride's family before the marriage can take place.

When a prospect is found, discreet inquiries are made about suitability. After the parents make their choice, the girl is asked for her agreement. Under Tunisian law, she has the right to refuse.

However, urban youth have increasing opportunity to meet and get to know one another independently. If a boy finds a girl he's interested in, he may ask a family member to approach her to see if she is receptive. If she is, female members of his family will call upon her family, and she will be closely observed. If she is deemed suitable, his mother will begin discussions with her mother, and the families will inquire further into each other's social standing and reputation. In most cases, parental consent is not absolutely necessary for a union to take place in Tunisia, but few young people will go against the wishes of their families.

When an engagement has been arranged, there is a big party to announce it. This is the first opportunity to celebrate publicly. The wedding rings are given during this ceremony. Although the couple may see each other after the public announcement, there is little opportunity, as they are busy with the preparations for the wedding.

The wedding events usually last from three to seven days. On the first day, the groom does the rounds with his male friends, buying gifts of clothes, jewelry, and perfumes for the bride. These are displayed in the quilted satin baskets you see for sale in Tunisia's *souqs*. He then, with great ceremony, delivers the gifts to the eagerly awaiting women of the bride's family.

On day two, the groom shaves off the beard he has been growing for a month. The bride has all her body hair "waxed" off with a sugar, water, and lemon paste, and her female friends apply intricate designs to her hands, arms, and feet using a paste made from henna leaves.

On the wedding day, the groom, with family
and friends, processes to the bride's home. A
ceremonial signing of the marriage contract, with
readings from the Koran, is held at the bride's
home, a hotel, or other venue, but not a mosque.
Many weddings are now held at the civil registry,
which provides a very attractive, low-key, and

cost-effective
alternative to a
lavish hotel
wedding,
where the
couple sit on
glitzy thrones,
sweating
under the
lights and
scrutiny of the crowd, and there is a seemingly
endless party. The bride may change her outfit
several times, wearing traditional dresses and a
Western-style gown.

At the end of the evening, the couple retire to
the man's house (nowadays usually a hotel), alone
together for the first time, for one week's seclusion
and consummation of the marriage. Thankfully,
women no longer wait outside for a bloodstained
sheet as proof of the bride's virginity.

Dealing with Illness
In Tunisian culture, health is considered to be a
blessing from God. People may believe that an
illness is a result of God's punishment, retribution
for doing wrong, being the victim of maliciously
intended magic, or offending or harming a *djinn*,

in addition to the usual medical explanations.

Tunisia has a modern health care system and modern alternative medicine, including acupuncture. In addition, there are traditional healers including bonesetters, dream interpreters, and herbalists.

Tunisians often seek mystical healing in a religious context. The shrines of certain saints are believed to have healing power. People will travel great distances to visit a shrine or special spa where it is believed that the place or the water may cure their ills.

Death

Burial usually takes place within a day of the death. The body is washed in rosewater and wrapped in a shroud. In Tunis, the body is placed in the living room, where visitors offer condolences before the burial. In Sfax, only direct family members can see the body, which is kept in the person's bedroom until it is taken to the cemetery. The body is laid in the grave with the feet facing Mecca.

Tunisians pray intensely for the mercy of Allah on the person's soul on the day of burial, as it is believed that one's judgment begins on that day. Family members gather to read from the Koran on the day of the death, the day of the funeral, and the following day. Readings also take place on each of the following three Wednesdays. Friends and relatives visit the family on each of the four Thursdays after the death. A final visit takes place on the fortieth day. Muslims believe that the soul lives on after physical death.

chapter six

TIME OUT

Tunisia may appear to be a fast-paced and work-oriented country, particularly from the vantage point of bustling, downtown Tunis, but Tunisians greatly value their holidays, vacations, and long lunch breaks. This is because they can spend more time with their family. As family takes precedence over work, employers are usually quite generous with vacation days.

Tunisians are extremely sociable. They enjoy

making new friends and rarely turn down an opportunity to get together. On their days off families like to visit relatives or friends. When Tunisians eat out, they do so in groups,

and in restaurants tables for six are much more common than tables for two.

Men (mainly) go to their favorite coffeehouse to play chess or *shkubbah*, a popular card game, to discuss sports and politics, conduct business, and, of course, drink coffee. At home people listen to music, watch videos or television, read, and relax. In nice weather they jam the beaches playing volleyball and football (soccer), the national pastime. Or they watch their favorite first division team—there are fourteen—live or on television.

They also become tourist-for-a-day at one of Tunisia's thousands of historical and archaeological sites. Popular day-trip destinations include the Great Mosque of Kairouan, one of Islam's holiest sites; the vast Roman amphitheater at El-Jem; and the mazelike cobblestone streets of the Sousse *medina*, built by the Aghlabids in the ninth century. There is also the world's largest collection of Roman mosaics in the spectacular setting of the former bey's palace, the Bardo Museum in Tunis.

Also in the Tunis area, the new Berges du Lac entertainment and commercial complex has become a popular destination. It has two bowling alleys, a water park, and an amusement park, restaurants ranging from fast food to elegant, and many stores selling local clothes and jewelry and Western brands ranging from Benetton to Max Mara. In Sousse, the huge, four-story Soula Shopping Center packs people in during their time off.

SHOPPING

Tunisia offers endless shopping options, from trendy boutiques and department stores to open-

air bazaars or *souqs*. *Souqs* are clusters of markets selling the same type of wares, such as carpets, household goods, auto parts, children's clothes, and handmade furniture. The *Souq al-Atarine* is the Perfume Makers' Souq. One of the largest *souqs* was the *Souq des Chechias,* where in the seventeenth century 15,000 craftsmen produced a million distinctive Tunisian red felt hats

(chechias) annually. Tunisians prefer to buy their spices and household goods in the *souq*.

Tunisia is the quintessential oriental bazaar, offering everything from deep-pile Berber rugs (*alloucha*), silver jewelry, fine gold chains, brass and copper bowls, trays, samovars and urns, to flowing robes, harem trousers, and diaphanous face veils (*yashmaks*) in the finest silks and chiffons. Decisions are difficult in the face of this vast choice, and for this reason shopping is best conducted at leisure, involving conversations, flattery, and lots of bargaining before a deal is finally struck.

Except for high-end imported luxury items favored by urban sophisticates, prices for most goods are reasonable.

BARGAINING

Prices in supermarkets and department stores are fixed, but bargaining is very much in evidence in bazaars and the *souq*. Being too eager raises the price, so, as a bargaining technique, don't ask about the item you like right away—inquire about something else first. Then, turn the shopkeeper's attention to the item you're interested in.

And here are two golden rules on the etiquette of bazaar bargaining:

Don't waste your and the seller's time haggling over something that costs very little. This is bad form.

Don't get into serious bargaining unless you intend to buy. Striking a deal is a verbal contract, and it is considered rude to come to an agreement over a price and then walk away without buying, especially if you have taken some time to bring the price down.

The best places for first-time visitors to Tunisia are the Artisanat (handicraft) shops, where everything is authentic and accurately priced. The carpets at the Artisanat are stamped for quality, reducing your chances of being cheated. Pure natural wool carpets, rugs, and shawls embroidered with the Hand of Fatima, Tree of Life, and other designs are extremely popular.

In the *souqs* one finds old coins, statues, perfumes, incense, art deco items, bric-à-brac, antique pottery, furniture, and artwork. Copper and brass plates and trays can be engraved on the spot in Arabic, and make a popular and inexpensive souvenir.

Besides shopping in the *souqs*, the weekly markets in the smaller towns and villages offer a variety of local specialties. Shopping amid jostling crowds of villagers buying and selling everything from animals to rough-hewn wooden kitchen utensils to coarse carpets and rural crafts can be good fun as well as an opportunity for bargain hunting.

As a general rule, plan on paying cash in the *souq*. Many vendors don't accept credit cards, and if they do, the commission will be passed on to

you. Also the vendor's idea of what a credit card charge is may differ from your own; you may find yourself being led to a bank branch where you are expected to draw cash against your credit card ("a cash advance") and pay the vendor. If you plan to pay by any means other than cash, work out the details early in the negotiation.

Also, when meeting Tunisians in the street in tourist areas, remember that, "my uncle has a good shop" probably means "I am employed by a particular shopkeeper to approach tourists and take them to his shop." Use your own judgment. Shopkeepers will constantly try to tempt you into their shops with promises of bargains and discounts.

FOOD

Tunisian cuisine has a long and noble lineage. The ingredients used today—grains, vegetables, olive oil, garlic, fruit, and seafood—are the same ones as depicted in Roman mosaics on view in the Bardo Museum. Tunisia's role in the early spice trade brought cumin, caraway, saffron, mustard, cayenne, ginger, cinnamon, dried rosebuds, black pepper, and sugar to the table. The Ottoman Turks imported the Persian style of combining meat, fruit, and cinnamon in a single dish. The Spanish introduced hot peppers to Tunisia; this is the main ingredient of *harissa*, the fiery red sauce made from crushed, dried chili, garlic, salt, and caraway seeds that is served with most dishes. Arabs, Jews, Andalusians, French, and Italians all added their bit to the mix. And to cap it all, the Berbers provided the Maghreb staple of couscous, a semolina-based pasta.

THE PERFECT COUSCOUS

Couscous is prepared by steaming semolina granules in a *couscousiere*, a two-piece pot. The upper part is a steamer for the couscous, while the sauce (tubers, squash, chickpeas, beef, chicken, lamb, or fish) cooks slowly underneath. The scented steam rises to cook the grains, which expand to up to three times their original size.

Breakfast

A typical Tunisian breakfast (*ftoor is-bah*) consists of milk, coffee, eggs, fritters, and *assida* (a pudding made with flour or semolina, oil, and dates). Those who want a lighter breakfast can seek out a patisserie for a croissant or *pain au chocolat* to go with their *café au lait*.

Lunch and Dinner

Lunch (*ftour*) is the biggest meal of the day, and dinner (*ashaa*) is comparatively light. This explains why the buses are so crowded at midday—people are rushing home to eat with their families.

A Tunisian meal usually starts with *kemia,* which are small, tasty dishes served as appetizers. Beside nuts, olives, *poutargue* (mullet roe), and spiced octopus, there are tingly crushed vegetable dishes such as spicy carrots, pumpkin, and courgette (zucchini), and *imalah* (pickled carrots and cauliflower). Perhaps Tunisia's favorite starter is the *salade mechouia*, a delicious blend of roasted peppers, garlic, and *harissa*. *Salade Tunisienne*, composed of finely chopped tomatoes, onion, and peppers, seasoned with lemon juice, olive oil, and mint, is also popular. The delicious o*mni houria*—cooked carrots mashed with garlic and olive oil—is served cold. A winter favorite is *chorba*, a piquant, tomato-based soup.

The *Briq*, a Tunisian curiosity of Middle Eastern origin, is a delicate deep-fried envelope of pastry that's usually filled with an egg skillfully cooked so that the white is set and the yolk is runny. It might be stuffed with onions, parsley, potato, capers, tuna, or meat.

Bread is eaten with every meal, ideally still warm from the local *boulangerie*. It's either a baguette (a long crusty French loaf) or, particularly in the countryside, *tabuna*. This traditional Berber bread is round, flat, and heavy, subtly flavored with *hab hlaoua* (aniseed) and named after the cylindrical clay oven in which it is baked.

For the main meat dishes, beef, lamb, or chicken may be prepared with tomatoes, potatoes, onions, and peppers, cooked with olive oil, spiced with aniseed, coriander, cumin, caraway, cinnamon, or saffron, and flavored with mint, orange blossom, or rosewater. A stew (*maraqa*) of meat, fruit, and spices is very popular, including *Maraquat al-Safarjal,* a delicious, slow-cooked sweet dish of lamb and quince—for which prunes or dried apricots may be substituted. For a more piquant dish try a lamb stew with chilis, tomatoes, or potatoes, spiced with paprika or cumin. The *maraqa*-style of cookery had a wide influence, and can be found in Provence, brought back by returned French settlers from North Africa. In Morocco, similar stews are called not *maraqa*, but *tajine*; but in Tunisia, a *tajine* is a kind of omelet. The explanation is that both stews and omelets are prepared in the shallow earthenware pot called a *tajine.* Lastly, the delicious *merguez*—spicy lamb or goat sausages—are almost as ubiquitous in Tunisia as *couscous.*

With its long coastline, Tunisia has excellent fresh seafood, including sole, red mullet, mackerel, grouper, perch, octopus, and squid. Favored seasonings are garlic, saffron, cumin, paprika, turmeric, or dried rosebuds (providing an aromatic rose-tinged flavor), though fish is often simply grilled with lemon or olive oil, or baked or fried in olive oil. Look out for *kabkabou,* an aromatic, tangy baked dish with saffron, preserved lemons, tomatoes, and capers, and simple, tasty fish *brochettes* (kebabs)—grilled chunks of fish and fresh vegetables. Mussels, clams, calamari, and prawns also feature widely. Succulent large prawns are grilled, sautéed with garlic and parsley, or simmered in a *gargoulette* (clay cooking pot).

When you think of Tunisia, think of Mediterranean sun-ripened fruits—figs, dates, oranges, peaches, pomegranates, and luscious grapes. In the interior, the prickly pear cactus—

imported by the Spanish in the sixteenth century from the Americas—is used to hedge in olive and almond groves. Small boys with long canes collect the attractive, yellow-orange, pear-shaped fruit at summer's end. Cactus fruit in the West is an expensive delicacy, but in Tunisia it's about the cheapest fruit you can find.

Almond cultivation in Tunisia dates back to the Punic-Roman period and currently averages about 6,000 tons a year, most of which is exported. The almond orchards around Sfax and Cap Bon provide the different almonds that are the basis of most Tunisian cakes and sweets.

Tunisian desserts are sweet, nutty, and delicious. Try *baklava* (sticky *filo* pastry filled with nuts and honey), *samsa* (*filo* pastry and ground almonds, baked in lemon and rosewater syrup), and *bouza* (hazelnut cream with grilled sesame seeds). *Makroud* (small, date-stuffed, honey-soaked wheat cakes) are a specialty of Kairouan.

DRINK
Coffee and Tea
Ahwa arbi (Turkish coffee), fragrant with orange blossom or rose water, is the drink of choice.

Other coffee variants include *express* (espresso), *café au lait* (with milk), or, for the faint-of-heart, Nescafe or other instant coffee.

Thé à la menthe (mint tea) is the classic North African drink, but one can also order *thé au pignon* (pine nuts) or *thé a l'almande* (with almonds).

Orange, grape, and other fruit juices are popular, and in many cafés are served freshly squeezed.

Citronade—lemon juice, water, and sugar—is a refreshing choice. Look out for seasonal juices or milkshakes with fresh fruit, but they may be sweeter than you like unless you ask for less sugar. And *lait de poule* is not "chicken's milk," but a fruit milkshake with egg white!

For a Muslim country, Tunisia's approach to alcohol is quite relaxed, in both the production and the consumption of alcoholic beverages. With alcohol being *haram* (forbidden) in Islam, retailers used to sell it behind the counter or in secluded areas. But recently hypermarket retailers, such as Monoprix and Carrefour, have taken to dedicating a specific store aisle to alcoholic beverages where products are visible and easy to reach. This new retailing trend makes it easier for consumers to take their time in making their purchase without feeling ashamed or ill at ease.

Tunisia produces a wide assortment of table wines, sparkling wines, beers, aperitifs, and local liqueurs. The most widely sold beer is the local lager, *Celtia*. *Boukh*, a sweet aromatic spirit distilled from figs, and *sarabi*, made from dates, are popular aperitifs. Aniseed drinks such as *pastis* are a throwback to the French era. Tunisia's red wines were the best under French rule, but now dry white Muscats are considered better. Rosés are the most consumed wines. Imported beer, wine, and spirits are considerably more expensive than the local products.

WHERE TO EAT AND DRINK
Fast-Food Places

There are no American-style fast-food restaurants, but authentically Tunisian, delicious sandwiches can be had at many of the g*argottes* (food stalls) along city streets. A sandwich favorite is the *casse-croute*, a jaw-challenging half-baguette, crammed with a selection of *harissa, salade mechouia*, cucumber, tomato, egg, tuna, and olives. Many waterfront g*argottes* offer delicious grilled fresh fish and vegetables. *Rotisseries* sell roast chicken, served piping hot with *pommes frites* (french fries). Simple roadside cafés (called *meshoui*) with smoky barbecues sell grilled lamb kebabs to hungry travelers. From the stack of brown-glazed terracotta bowls, you can spot the places that offer *lablabi*, a filling chickpea, *harissa*, and cumin soup poured over broken bread—perfect for cold winter mornings.

Restaurants

Tunis boasts eateries of every description, including French, Italian, and other international restaurants. Other towns and cities have a decent range of restaurants, with French food on offer just about everywhere. Prices vary enormously, with higher prices not necessarily meaning a better meal.

Restaurants touristiques are not just for tourists. They're graded by the National Tourist Office (ONT), marked with one, two, or three forks, serve Tunisian and international specialties, and are licensed to serve alcohol.

One dining hazard is cigarette smoke in restaurants. There are few nonsmoking areas, and these may or may not be respected. Asking a Tunisian to put out his cigarette would be considered rude, and it wouldn't have much effect because there are too many smokers to contend with. The best advice is for you to pick your dining spot carefully—perhaps outside on the patio—and eat early, before the crowds arrive.

TIPPING

Tipping is not generally expected in cafés and local restaurants, but underpaid waiters will appreciate anything you give them. A saucer is usually provided for customers to throw in their small change. In tourist restaurants, however, waiters are accustomed to tips— 10 percent is plenty. Taxi drivers do not usually expect tips, but appreciate them.

Bars and Cafés

Most bars are raucous, smoky, all-male preserves.
For a more salubrious drink in a place where
women will feel comfortable, head for a reputable
hotel bar or a restaurant.

Cafés range from stand-up
patisseries fit for a quick coffee and
pastry to leisurely, male-dominated
gossip havens, where the clientele
plays games of cards, backgammon,
chess, or dominoes. Some smoke
tobacco water pipes, known as
sheesha or *nargila*. These
contraptions cool the fragrant
smoke, making for a gentle puff with attendant
musical gurgle; you can have *mwassi* (honey-
soaked) or *tufa* (apple-flavored) tobacco. Some
cafés have a mixed clientele, particularly in Tunis,
and there are a few ladies-only cafés.

LEISURE
Music

Tunisians love music, and there are endless
concerts to go to. The Carthage International
Festival is celebrating its forty-fourth summer
season. Concerts take place in the spectacular
open-air Roman theater, which seats 7,500
spectators. In addition to noted Arab performers,
over the years the festival has attracted Miriam
Makeba, James Brown, Youssou Ndour, Louis
Armstrong, Ray Charles, and Joe Cocker.

Lovers of classical music are not neglected in
Tunisia. One can attend concerts at the

International Symphonic Music Festival in the sandstone Roman amphitheater at El-Jem or in the Roman theater at Dougga, both within a few hours' drive of Tunis. A new classical musical venue is the Acropolium, the deconsecrated nineteenth-century Catholic cathedral of Carthage, which hosts a music festival in October that attracts performers and audiences from all over the world.

Another musical option is the western seaside town of Tabarka, which hosts jazz, Latin, world music, and *Rai* musical festivals during the summer. *Rai* updates traditional Arab sounds with a pop beat. French *Rai* superstars meet up with their Algerian cousins in the relaxed ambience of Tabarka.

Tunisian classical music, or *malouf* (meaning "normal"), is called the "emblem of Tunisia's national identity." *Malouf* was brought to Tunisia in the fifteenth century by Andalusian refugees who played in small ensembles using a *rbab* (a two-stringed kind of violin), *oud* (lute) and *darbuka* (drum), with a solo vocalist. *Malouf* underwent a revival in the 1930s when Baron d'Erlanger, a musicologist living in Sidi Bou Said, founded the Rachidia Institute. This is where most of Tunisia's leading musicians have trained and it is still Tunisia's best place to hear classical music. At the baron's mansion you can find his six-volume treatise of the rules and history of *malouf* and see his collection of musical instruments.

Cinema

Tunisia has a small, internationally renowned film industry—but one wouldn't know it from the mix offered at Tunisian cinemas. It's easier to see good Tunisian films in art houses and film festivals abroad than at local cinemas, where the usual fare is a mix of Hollywood blockbusters dubbed in French, Bollywood spectaculars, and Egyptian slapstick. One happy exception to the above occurs in October at the biennial Carthage Film Festival, where internationally recognized Tunisian films are on offer.

One of Tunisia's most notable films is *The Silence of the Palace* (*Samt al Qasr*), directed and written in 1994 by Moufida Tlatli, which deals with the beginning of the struggle for women's emancipation in Tunisia. Another Tunisian classic is Férid Boughedir's *A Summer in La Goulette* (1995), which chronicles Claudia Cardinale's (real-life) return to her childhood home in Tunisia at the time that the 1967 Arab–Israeli War was destroying much of the multiethnic ambience of Tunisia.

Two major international productions—*Star Wars* (1977) and *The English Patient* (1996)—were filmed in Tunisia.

Theater

The theater season lasts from October to June, when two companies present a series of six to eight well-known French-language plays. Performances take place at the Municipal Theater in Tunis, with its striking Art Nouveau facade, and the National Theater, situated at the restored

Khaznadar Palace at Bab Souika. Plays are also given at La Goulette, Carthage, Hammamet, Gabès, Gafsa, and Sousse.

Belly Dancing

Belly dancing is a Western term for the sexy Middle Eastern dance form (*raqs sharqi*), which may originally have been a fertility rite. Tunisians have a conflicted relationship with belly dancing. On the one hand, they consider it a national art, and many families hire belly dancers as

Satin Rouge

The Tunisian film director Raja Amari, who lives and works in Paris, won an award at the Seattle Film Festival in 2002 for her feature-length movie *Satin Rouge.* This is the story of a widowed Tunisian housewife who, tired of living in the shadow of her daughter and dead husband, finds herself drawn to the seductive, but socially unacceptable, belly dance cabaret down the street.

entertainers at wedding parties. Men, women, and children cheer the belly dancer on at such gatherings, and encourage young girls to join her on the dance floor. On the other hand, belly dancers are considered loose, and their world sleazy. "Nice girls" don't want to be belly dancers.

SPORTS
The National Game

Tunisian men are crazy about football (soccer). The Tunisian national team is one of the strongest teams in Africa, having qualified for the World Cup finals in 1978, 1998, 2002, and 2006. Tunisia hosted the 2004 African Cup of Nations, and won the tournament!

You will impress Tunisians if you know something about their first division teams. *Esperance Sportive de* Tunisie (Tunis) and *Etoile Sportif du Sahel* (Sousse) usually dominate the local competition. Club matches are held from early October until the end of March, usually on Saturday and Sunday afternoons.

Football is also a family sport and has been important in creating a demand for satellite television. In summer, many a street and even the beach is a football playing field.

Other Sports
Tunisian runners have achieved international success in middle- and long-distance track and field competitions. Tourism has provided resources for the development of other sports,

including tennis, golf, hiking, and windsurfing. Scuba diving has benefited from a vigorous conservation program designed to protect underwater flora and fauna. Wild boar hunting is popular in the hills and mountains near Tabarka. Tunisian women actively participate in sports, unlike those in some other Muslim countries, and have distinguished themselves in football, tennis, and gymnastics.

SPA TREATMENTS

Thalassotherapy, a homeopathic treatment involving seawater developed in France in the nineteenth century, is very popular with tourists and Tunisians alike. The Mediterranean waters that are the balm of the French are the main ingredient of Tunisia's treatments. At Tunisian spas one is doused in showers of warmed seawater, caked in mud-and-seaweed wrappings, and enveloped in a mist of sea fog.

Chemical elements found in seawater are believed to be absorbed through the skin, supposedly relieving the effects of hypertension, bronchitis, muscle atrophy, and arthritic symptoms. Although the medical benefits of thalassotherapy have yet to be scientifically proven, its adherents are not shy about extolling its virtues.

THE *HAMMAM*

As Tunisians traditionally had no baths or showers in their homes, the *hammam,* or public bathhouse, was the place to wash while meeting your friends. Even with the advent of indoor plumbing, the appeal of the *hammam* is still strong, particularly in winter as a way to escape a drafty apartment. Every town in Tunisia has at least one *hammam*, with Tunis having some of the most historic and best ones. You can spot them by their red and green candy-striped doorways and undecorated domes.

Hammams handle segregation of the sexes in different ways: there may be separate sections or different times for men and women; there may also be men-only and women-only *hammams*. But, rest assured, men and women do not share the same space at the same time.

The standard service includes a rubdown with a *kassa*, a coarse mitten, which removes dead skin after your stint in the steam room. A massage costs a little extra, but be aware that it is much more vigorous than is usual in the West. You should bring a towel and shorts for moving around the *hammam*, because nudity is not practiced. Make sure you have something dry to put on afterward.

chapter seven

TRAVEL, HEALTH, & SAFETY

Tunisia is a traveler's delight, with its long
Mediterranean coastline, hills and mountains, oak
forests, high plateau, and desert. For the history
buff there are numerous archaeological and
historical sites. All this is temptingly accessible.
The transport infrastructure is excellent, and
there are lodgings of every description. Prices are
reasonable, the people are friendly and helpful,
and the travel experience is enjoyable and
memorable. There is absolutely no reason for the
visitor *not* to explore the whole country!

ROADS AND DRIVING

Well-maintained, paved roads connect all major
towns and cities, and it's easy to move around the
country. Even minor roads are now being paved,
particularly in the south where the army has been
heavily involved in road building. The only toll
road (*péage*) is the new and inexpensive
expressway that links Tunis and Sousse.

Police officers rarely stop foreigners, but it's
best to ensure you have your passport, driver's
license, and car registration papers handy at all
times. International and foreign driver's licenses
are accepted in Tunisia. The British AA and RAC

are affiliated to the National Automobile Club (NACT) based in Tunis. Insurance valid for up to twenty-one days can be purchased at the border. In the case of a breakdown, the *Garde Nationale* (National Guard) will assist free of charge; they usually contact the nearest garage.

In Tunisia you drive on the right side of the road. Tunisians drive fairly safely, though they frequently pass with little regard for what's coming from the opposite direction. Perhaps greater hazards for the newcomer are the moped riders who weave in and out of traffic, and the pedestrians who think they have a God-given right to walk on the road regardless of traffic. In country towns, watch out for farm animals and small children. Drive defensively.

The regulation that causes most problems for visitors is the *priorité à droite,* the rule requiring a driver to yield to traffic coming from the right, even when on a traffic circle.

Car rental is available from major international agencies as well as smaller Tunisian companies, which are usually cheaper. Fuel is inexpensive by European standards.

INTERCITY TRAVEL

Tunisia has a well-developed, efficient transportation network consisting of air travel, trains, buses, shared taxis *(louages)*, and ferries. Crossing by ferry from Italy or France is a popular option, with year-round service. There are six airports handling international and domestic traffic. Just about every location in the country has daily connections with Tunis.

Trains
The state-owned Société Nationale des Chemins de Fer Tunisiens (SNCFT) operates the railway network. Although not all parts of the country are linked, train travel is generally modern, efficient, and comfortable—as long as you can get a seat.

The main route is between Tunis and Gabès, via Sousse, Sfax, and Gafsa. Eight daily trains ply this route, many with air-conditioned coaches and a buffet. Unless you're traveling on this main line route, you're usually better off taking a bus or a *louage*.

Those who are seeking a scenic day out should consider taking the *Lézard Rouge* (Red Lizard), a restored train of the former bey, that wends its way though the mountains, offering great views of the Seldja Gorge.

Buses
The Société Nationale du Transport Rural et Interurbain (SNTRI, pronounced "sintry") operates

daily air-conditioned buses to just about every place in the country. These buses run pretty much on schedule, and they're comfortable and inexpensive. In summer, buses run at night to avoid the scorching daytime temperatures. The efficiency of the service means that they're always full, so it's advisable to book ahead, particularly in summer.

There are many companies for regional buses, which may be your only form of transportation to the smaller towns. They may operate from the same terminal as the SNTRI buses, so be careful to get on the right bus. Your bus may be very salubrious and comfortable, or it may be poorly maintained, overcrowded, and malodorous, with villagers toting fruit, vegetables, and live chickens—it's hard to predict. As a general proposition, one can say that the regional buses are fairly reliable, but they are slower than the SNTRI buses, and never air-conditioned. Your fellow-travelers will be friendly, and you may have an memorable travel experience.

Louages

You can find *louage* stations all over Tunisia, and these long-distance, shared taxis are a fast, friendly, and convenient way to get around. Usually Mercedes, Peugeot, or Renault station wagons, they normally carry up to five passengers, leaving when they are full, to no fixed schedule. Fares are quoted *par place* (per person), and are similar to those on buses and trains. There are no discounts for children. There may be a small charge for luggage.

LOCAL TRANSPORTATION
Buses
The local state-run yellow bus network in Tunis is ridiculously cheap, but buses are jammed with commuters not only in the mornings and evenings but at midday too, when workers hurry home to be with their families for lunch. Another option, nearly as cheap, is the green (private) bus network connecting the business districts with the larger residential areas of Tunis. Comparable local bus networks operate in other Tunisian cities.

Light Rail
In Tunis, a streetcar network (the *metro léger*) crisscrosses the city, with five main routes. The trains are inexpensive and easy to use. You buy your ticket at the small kiosks at each station entrance. There is also a suburban train line (TGM) that links Tunis with the beachside northern suburbs.

Taxis
Taxis can be found in all but the smallest towns and are not expensive—though you may need to ask the driver to turn on the meter if he "forgets." Be warned that the meter may seem confusing at first, because the currency has so many digits: a fare of TD 3.5 is displayed as 03,500. When the meter is not used—for example, on a trip to the suburbs—agree on the price beforehand.

Most taxi drivers obey traffic signals and observe the speed limits. Many visitors report pleasant, and sometimes memorable, encounters with drivers, who are usually friendly and willing to talk endlessly about their country and their children in Arabic, French, and occasionally broken English, to the accompaniment of loud Arabic music. Occasionally one hears of a disagreeable encounter with a cab driver, and this will probably be because of a dispute over the fare when the meter was not turned on and a price was not agreed to beforehand.

Tipping taxi drivers is not customary, though a tip for good service will be appreciated.

WHERE TO STAY

For expatriates seeking permanent housing, Tunis and its residential suburbs usually head the list of best places to live in Africa. This is based on the high quality and reasonable cost of housing, the low crime rate, and the relatively benign sociocultural environment. Because of better amenities, most foreigners choose a villa or apartment in the *ville nouvelle* instead of the *medina.*

As for hotels, there is plenty of choice, from five-star chains to inexpensive backpacker places. Even small towns usually have lodging options in different price ranges. Tunisian hotels fall into two main categories: classified establishments, awarded from one to five stars by the government; and those not classified. Hotels in the latter group are indicated by the initials NC (*nonclassifié*)

and include some in pleasant, even charming, spots.

Hotel prices are normally listed according to the three seasons—high, middle, and low. The high season usually corresponds to the European summer and the Christmas vacation period. The low season is from November 1 to March 15 (excluding Christmas), and the periods between form the middle season.

It is quite acceptable to ask to see a room before deciding to stay, and in smaller hotels it is possible to bargain, particularly if the type of room you want is not available or the room is flawed in some way. Be sure to ask if there are any discounts, as these are rarely advertised.

HEALTH

Good health care is available in the larger cities where many doctors are foreign-trained and speak English. Things are much more hit-or-miss in rural areas. The country has a good nationwide system of health clinics, though nursing care may be limited or rudimentary as this is something that family or friends are expected to provide.

An important part of the health care system is the nationwide availability of pharmacies. Unlike in the USA, pharmacists are authorized to diagnose minor conditions and sell medicines without a prescription. They can also advise on specialist help and recommend good local clinics.

Reciprocal arrangements with countries rarely exist, and you should expect to pay for all medical expenses immediately upon treatment. The costs may be less than you are used to, but medical insurance is always advisable.

If you take regular medication, bring adequate supplies with you. What you need may not be available in Tunisia. If you have a chronic condition or a medicinal allergy, it is important to know how to discuss it in French or Arabic, or at least carry information about your condition in French on your person at all times.

As to dentistry, except for Tunis and the larger cities, standards vary. It's best to have dental work done before coming to Tunisia, as there may be increased risks of Hepatitis B and HIV transmission via poorly sterilized equipment.

Precautions

There are some standard dos and don'ts for staying healthy in Tunisia. Before coming to the country, seek advice from your medical practitioner on inoculations and other precautions; this is particularly important if you are intending to stay for some time.

It's best not to drink tap water, at least until you've allowed your body a period of adjustment. Bottled water is cheap and widely available. Avoid uncooked vegetables when eating out, and be sure to ask for meat to be *bien cuite.*

Hepatitis A, spread through contact with contaminated food or water, is present in Tunisia, and precautions should be taken, particularly in rural areas. Hepatitis B is also there, and anyone who has intimate contact with Tunisians should be tested regularly.

Various intestinal infections are common. If you do develop diarrhea, it is important to keep hydrated—drink plenty of fluids. If you suffer a severe attack, you should see a doctor.

HIV exists in Tunisia, though it is far below the epidemic proportions found south of the Sahara. Documented HIV/AIDS cases total nearly 9,000. Men account for three-quarters of this number, and most cases are in the Tunis metropolitan area. Drug use is responsible for most cases among men, followed by heterosexual and homosexual conduct. For women, heterosexual activity is the main cause, and drug use is not statistically important. On the whole, people are well-informed about AIDS. To be prudent, any visitor should practice safe sex meticulously.

SAFETY
Terrorism
After 9/11 and the terrorist attack in Jerba in April 2002, the government took strict measures to counter the threat. Metal detectors were installed at the entrances to all tourist sites and hotels. Police monitor areas frequented by foreigners. While there is currently no specific threat directed against foreigners, travelers are urged to be vigilant and follow the advice provided by embassies or hotels.

Crime
By Western standards, the crime rate is low. Most crimes are purse snatching, theft of unattended property, and pickpocketing in tourist areas like the *medinas* of Tunis and Sousse. Just take normal precautions with your belongings.

Acts of violence are rare, and visitors often describe how safe they feel walking around, day or night. However, in July 2008, the resort town of Port El Kantaoui was rocked by the brutal murder of a Englishwoman. A Tunisian man was arrested, and the crime received a great deal of attention because it was such a rare occurrence.

Harassment of Women

Foreign women are often misunderstood by conservative Tunisians. Friendliness may be misinterpreted as flirtation, and women out at night without a male escort can give the impression that they are inviting attention, which can lead to harassment. Most Tunisian women do not show legs, bare arms, or cleavage when out and about, and visitors are advised to follow their example. If you are going to a Western-style establishment where revealing clothes are acceptable, wear a large shawl or coat on the journey there and back.

Most harassment takes the form of whistling, leering, or even groping. Some people say that the woman should shout a response at the harasser in Arabic, but this is unwise. She should not interact with the aggressor: it will not shame him into stopping, and is likely to provoke laughter and more harassment. She can either shout to attract attention and scare the offender off, or simply walk away from the situation. Harassment rarely takes place at tourist resorts or beaches, where people are used to mingling with foreigners.

chapter eight

BUSINESS BRIEFING

Banks, businesses, and foreign embassies in Tunisia have a Western-style working week, and take Saturday and Sunday off. Government and public-sector institutions work full-time Monday through Thursday, and shortened hours (until 1:00 p.m.) on Friday and Saturday, allowing the faithful to attend Friday prayers and begin their weekend on Saturday afternoon.

Tunis and the major towns and cities have excellent business facilities. Business centers and rooms at the large hotels have satellite TV, fax machines, printing facilities, and high-speed Internet connections. This modern infrastructure may give you the impression that the business differences between Tunisia and the West are negligible, but this would not be strictly true.

BUSINESS CULTURE

When you are doing business with Tunisians, keep their core values in mind. Preserving honor and saving face, both for oneself and for the other party, are key. Tunisians want to know you and like you before conducting business with you, and people and good relationships are more important than time. This makes negotiations lengthy.

The support system that Tunisians rely on is provided by their social network, including family, school friends, and neighbors. It is all about contacts. Calling old friends for favors and pulling strings is the norm. Connections are the key to getting a good job, sometimes *any* job. Personal recommendations take one much further than qualifications on paper.

For a foreigner, the best way to build a network is to develop a relationship with someone who already has good contacts. You will then be introduced as a friend. Nurturing this first relationship takes time. It involves getting to know the other party, calling regularly, asking how things are going, and generally being helpful. Many foreigners fail to realize that this is how business happens: time spent developing a relationship is not  wasted, but opens doors to future success. Once a relationship is established, people will often put themselves out to help you achieve your objective.

The US Department of State advises that, "Good local agents/distributors are usually crucial to introducing products into Tunisia. Knowledge of the local market and local contacts can mean the difference between success and failure." (*Country Commercial Guide for Tunisia.*)

It is important to be patient with regard to Tunisian timekeeping. It is true that being punctual indicates seriousness, but time is flexible in Tunisia, and "on time" is a relative concept.

THE LANGUAGE OF BUSINESS

Arabic is the first language of Tunisia, and proficiency in it will gain you respect; but French is the language of business. If you don't speak either language, and if you haven't arranged for an interpreter to accompany you, you may have an unproductive meeting. Establish in advance what the language of the meeting will be, and ensure language support if necessary.

"SWEETENERS"

In a society of patronage and hierarchy, where connections are all-important, the potential for corruption is considerable. So it is not surprising that Transparency International, the civil society organization leading the fight against global corruption, finds in the 2007 *Corruption Perception Index* that corruption is a serious problem in Tunisia—though it is below the levels in many Arab and African countries. The study notes that cronyism and influence peddling may have affected some investment decisions in the past.

To get something done in Tunisia, a number of licenses, clearances, or permits may be required. This may lead to some form of bribery or kickback being exacted at different stages in the approval process. Detailed provisions in Tunisia's penal code prohibit bribery and corruption, though there seems little indication to date that these provisions have had much impact in changing ingrained cultural practices.

BUSINESS ETIQUETTE

In a nutshell—be courteous, expect formality, observe protocol, and show respect.

Since harmony is highly valued, you should stay cool, speak moderately, and always maintain self-control. Your demeanor will be carefully noted.

Expect the business setting to be formal, even exaggeratedly so, because Tunisians want to give international visitors the best possible impression of their culture. Let the Tunisians take the first step to put relations on a more relaxed footing.

You should observe protocol by understanding the hierarchy of your environment and respecting seniority.

Show respect by addressing a person by his or her correct title. Find out the person's correct title before the meeting. Anyone with a doctorate will expect to be called "Doctor."

Business Dress

Tunisians tend to judge others on appearances, so it is in your best interests to dress well and pay attention to detail, such as ensuring your shoes are well polished. Business dress is generally sober and formal. Dark, classic suits with conservative ties are

the norm for men. In the heat of summer, it is often possible to dispense with the jacket, although it is best to err on the side of formality and follow the lead of your Tunisian hosts.

For women, elegant but conservative suits, dresses, or pantsuits are best. It is important to be appropriately covered, with long sleeves and skirts below the knee (worn with hose or tights). Clothes should not be tight fitting, and jackets that cover the hips are advised; a sharp pantsuit with a long jacket is ideal. Accessories should be minimal and not ostentatious. Designer labels are highly regarded, and even casual dress should be snappy.

Business Cards

Business cards are exchanged without formal ritual. They should be bilingual, in Arabic and French. When presenting cards at a meeting, start with the highest-ranking Tunisian.

Credentials impress Tunisians. So if you have an advanced university degree from a prestigious university or have achieved special recognition in your business field, try to weave this information into the discussion in a non-boastful way.

Business Gifts

There is a certain protocol to gift giving. It is important not to be excessively generous, as "a gift demands a gift." Appropriate gifts include elegant stationery, framed photos of a significant business-related event, or crafts from your own country. In short, anything that makes a thoughtful personal link between the two of you is a good business gift. If invited for a meal, elegantly presented pastries, dates, or figs are excellent gifts, as are small items for children.

LEADERSHIP AND DECISION MAKING

Tunisian business is top-down. Protocol is important and the hierarchical code demands great respect for the person in charge. The highest-ranking person makes the decisions, after obtaining group consensus. Tunisians will not generally contradict their superiors, and may tell them what they think they want to hear. It is generally accepted that the person in charge will give specific instructions, and these instructions and limits of authority will be followed carefully. Bounds are rarely overstepped, and honest input can be hard to come by.

Lengthy deliberation over decisions is the norm, and at times it may seem that no one wants to accept responsibility for finding the solution. Innovation and bold speech are in general not favorably regarded. Government negotiations entail more protocol and political maneuvering to be sure that all the relevant officials have been consulted and positions respected, and several meetings may be required to accomplish even simple things. This may all take more time and patience than you wish, but remember that Tunisians tend to be conservative and interested in long-term relationships.

MEETINGS AND NEGOTIATIONS

Appointments are necessary, and should be made as far in advance as possible and confirmed a day or two before the meeting. It is also wise to schedule yourself loosely, often not more than a few meetings a day. Allow time for lateness, missed appointments, and delays in completing or accomplishing things. A good rule of thumb is to be prompt yourself, but flexible about punctuality in others.

Make an attempt to learn in advance the full names of people who will attend a meeting, because it may be hard to assimilate this information at the meeting. Names may be rattled off quickly, last name first. Also, confusingly, people often introduce themselves by their first name, while everyone else calls them by their last name. A basic familiarity with Arab names may make your task easier and help you to remember names. Use formal address unless invited to do otherwise. *Sidi* is the respectful form of address, equivalent to "Mr."

Allow time for courtesies and small talk. A simple chat can result in opportunities for other introductions or contacts—which are best seized at the moment. If you don't take immediate advantage of an opportunity it may be lost forever.

Tea and coffee are likely to be served early and often during the meeting. Expect interruptions, as an open-door policy is generally observed, and others may join you to discuss unrelated matters. Be patient, and don't try to redirect the discussion to the original topic until the newcomer leaves.

You will encounter Tunisians who are strict in their religious observances, and those who are not. It is obligatory for a Muslim to pray five times a day, and it is courteous and respectful to allow space and time for this practice. If someone steps away from a meeting to pray, simply carry on your business quietly and resume without comment when your companion returns.

Although Tunisians can be shrewd and skillful negotiators, and may pressure you, high-pressure tactics on your part tend to backfire.

PRESENTATIONS

Presentations are an increasingly common ingredient of business meetings. In the private sector, the atmosphere is comparable to Western-style presentations, where disruptions are unlikely and time constraints apply. In dealing with the government or traditional family businesses, older customs remain, and you are likely to be interrupted frequently by phone calls, people bringing in papers for signature, and other comings and goings. This does not mean that your business is unimportant, but people are used to juggling many things at once. If a senior person receives a phone call during your presentation, stop, and resume when he is ready. Be patient.

The time allotted to you will depend very much on whom you are meeting: the more senior the person, the less time you will have. It is wise to ask beforehand how much time will be available to you in order to prepare appropriately; you may have anything between fifteen minutes and an hour. Generally, it is middle management or heads of department who attend presentations—rarely will the top decision maker be there. If the company chief is present, get straight to the point; otherwise spend the first five or ten minutes on introductions and conversation.

During the presentation, personal anecdotes and stories are not advisable, nor are jokes. Tunisians do not always relate to Western humor, but if a foreigner makes a joke they will be forced to laugh to avoid embarrassing him. Joking in a presentation setting creates awkwardness.

Usually questions come at the end, and are polite and indirect. Sensitive issues may best be dealt with privately. Audiovisual aids and handouts impress, and suggest seriousness and preparation, but be careful to avoid ostentation or anything that may make others believe that you are trying to outdo them or make them feel inferior.

CONTRACTS

Commitments in Tunisia are looser than they are in the West, and unfulfilled promises are endemic in the Arab world. This fact should be carefully considered when moving to the contract stage.

Contract and property laws are well developed, deriving from the French Napoleonic Code. However, in this relationship-based society, a contract may not hold up if there is a fundamental lack of trust between the parties. Because of the length and complexity of legal procedures, and the fact that the judiciary is not fully independent of the executive branch, one should consult carefully with a Tunisian lawyer before entering into any contract or agreement. The US Department of State, in its *Country Commercial Guide for Tunisia*, states, "To avoid misunderstanding, contracts for investment projects should always contain a clause detailing how eventual disputes should be handled and the applicable jurisdiction. Tunisia is a member of the International Center for the Settlement of Investment Disputes and a signatory to the 1958 New York Convention on the Recognition and Enforcement of Foreign Arbitral Awards."

CANDOR AND COOPERATION

The importance placed on saving face may challenge the Western concept of honesty. For example, a secretary may tell a white lie about her boss to protect his honor, such as, "Habib is busy on the telephone," when in fact he is late for work. If you let on that you realize this, it would be an affront both to Habib and to his secretary.

This principle works both ways. For fear of offending your honor, Tunisians are unlikely to let you know that they think your claims are exaggerated or that they don't believe you will be able to keep to the schedule you have promised. It is important to ask them if they have any questions or doubts, and to make sure they realize you will not be offended by hearing their true thoughts.

It is rare to hear a Tunisian say, "I don't know." This would entail a loss of face, so rather than saying it outright, they may give you their best guess. A direct "No" is also uncommon—instead, a person may avoid or change the subject in order not to offend. This is particularly true when others are present. If you sense this is happening, save your question for someone more senior, or ask it in a letter or e-mail, so they will have a chance to research it before replying.

Tunisians do not like to give bad news. In response to a question about a promised product or report, you are likely to get the reply, "It's nearly ready," even if the work has only just been started. If you leave a meeting having been told, "Give us a sample and we will test it and place an order next month," it might mean just that, or it might mean, "This is too expensive/the wrong color/no good, but we don't want to ruin your day by telling you," and the awaited order will never materialize.

"*Mashi mushkil*" ("no problem") is a phrase one hears often. It should be taken with a grain of salt. It is not uncommon for these to be the last words you hear from someone who then avoids you because he cannot fulfill his commitments.

TEAMWORK AND MANAGEMENT
Go slow! As part of a team, allow time for people to trust you before suggesting change. Take care to listen to everyone and to respect their ideas. Don't ever dismiss an idea in public; if you do, the person who ventured it will never suggest another idea to you for fear of losing face.

Ultimately, the boss is the boss; the manager has clear authority to make the final decision, and the team will swing in behind him, even if they don't agree with it. People are more concerned with group success, and keeping the group together, than appearing to be the individual shining star. This has its pros and cons. If a problem arises, don't expect anyone to take responsibility, especially in public. Blame shifting is widely practiced. More time may be spent in placing blame than in resolving the problem.

WOMEN IN MANAGEMENT

Women in managerial positions are well respected. Male visitors should be polite and respectful, avoid excessive eye contact, and shake hands only if the woman offers hers first. Physical contact may not be acceptable if she is strictly religious. Formal address (*Madame* or *Mademoiselle* with the family name) should be used.

Do not expect female colleagues to attend evening meetings except in liberal urban areas. Many women prefer to return home early at night to avoid the stigma of *hishma* that could occur if they were seen returning late.

chapter **nine**

COMMUNICATING

LANGUAGE

Arabic is Tunisia's official language—but, as elsewhere in the Arab world, the spoken language differs greatly from the written language. There are two varieties of written Arabic. The first is classical Arabic, the language of the Koran, and the second is standard Arabic, the language of the mass media, government, and literature. The spoken language is Darija, or Tunsi, the Tunisian variant of Arabic spoken in the Maghreb. The most immediately apparent difference between Tunisian and standard Arabic is the large number of words borrowed from French, Italian, Spanish, Berber, and Turkish that make Tunsi almost a separate language. Berber, North Africa's indigenous language, is spoken in only a few parts of the extreme south.

Tunsi grew as an oral tradition, kept alive by wandering storytellers and bards at marketplaces and festivals, but its use has diminished since the widespread introduction of television and the mass media. Most novels or short stories are in standard Arabic or French, except for dialect, which may be written in Tunsi. Plays are often written in Tunsi, except when they are placed in a historical setting. The lyrics to folk and popular music are usually in Tunsi.

The use of Tunisian Arabic in literary fields is generally not readily accepted. A 1997 translation into Tunsi of Antoine de Saint-Exupéry's *Le Petit Prince* was greeted with much criticism by those who felt it was a threat to the national written language of the country.

تونس

Newspapers and magazines are printed either in French or in standard Arabic. Television newscasts and documentaries are broadcast in standard Arabic, while locally produced soap operas, sitcoms, and movies are usually in Tunsi.

In addition to Arabic, French is spoken in business and official circles, and is also used in scientific disciplines. A growing number of young people speak some English, since it is considered imperative to national and individual success, and is taught in schools.

MANNERS

In Tunisia, as in much of the Arab world, attitude overrides vocabulary. Good manners envelop every interaction. Tunisians are helpful by nature. If asked for something, they must oblige. And sometimes they will do so even when not asked. For example, ask for directions in the street and, before you know it, a crowd has gathered and is engaged in earnest debate about the best possible route for you.

In conversation, good posture is important. Slouching shows a lack of respect. Putting your feet up or crossing your legs in a way that exposes the soles of your shoes is considered rude, especially in front of seniors. In a group setting, it is rude to present your back to someone. If you have to do so, for whatever reason, you should apologize to the person.

The sense of personal space in Tunisia differs from that in the West. People tend to sit closer to each other and may be more tactile, but not with the opposite sex. Don't back away—this would make you appear cold or imply that you find the other person offensive.

NONVERBAL COMMUNICATION

Touching between members of the same sex is common to emphasize speech and communicate warmth. Thus members of the same sex will normally kiss one another on each cheek when greeting, with women often drawing this out to three or four kisses. However, a man and woman do not hold hands in public because public displays of affection between the sexes are inappropriate. This is different for the urban young , who greet close friends of the opposite sex with a kiss on the cheek.

A handshake between men frequently lasts throughout the entire conversation. Same-sex friends walking together quite often hold hands or link arms; this is simply friendship, and does not in any way indicate a homosexual relationship.

As in other Arab societies, it is important to be careful with one's left hand, which is used for personal hygiene. Tunisians who are born left-handed tend to write with their left hand but learn to use only the right hand for shaking hands, passing objects, touching others, and eating.

However, not all Tunisians subscribe to the tradition of avoiding use of the left hand. Many urbanites use both hands freely.

Hand gestures are important. Tunisians, like other Mediterranean people, are spirited in conversational gestures and appreciate the same from visitors.

GESTURES AND TABOOS

- A shrug of the shoulders expresses the feeling "What can I do about it?"
- After shaking hands, Tunisians may put their right hand over their heart for a moment, to indicate sincerity.
- Two index fingers placed side by side indicate *kif-kif*, or same, and can also imply friendship or a relationship.
- Waving with the palm toward the body, with the thumb and all fingertips pulled together and pointing up, can mean "good" or "wait," depending on the context.
- You beckon by waving all fingers toward the body with the palm facing down.
- You can use the index finger to point at an object, but not at people. Generally, it is better to place the index finger under the middle finger and point with both.
- Many Tunisians consider it inappropriate to wink at someone in public, though it is fairly common among the young.
- Creating a circle with the thumb and index finger, which means "OK" in many countries, means "zero" or "bad" in Tunisia.

THE MEDIA

While there is no official censorship of the media, the government retains a tight hold on local broadcasting and the press. Self-censorship is practiced, as various types of government coercion have restricted the ability of journalists and political personalities to speak freely. Nonetheless, the high rate of literacy and the sizable middle class have helped to sustain an avid readership for the large number of periodicals covering such subjects as arts and culture, sports, hometown news, business, and economics. In addition, radio and TV have large followings.

Radio and Television

Local radio stations broadcast in both French and Arabic on standard AM frequencies. The state-run Tunisian Radio and the privately owned Radio Mosaique are the principal broadcasters. There is a daily hour of English-language radio on RTCI (Radio Tunis Chaine Internationale), the local FM station, which also broadcasts in French, German, Italian, and Spanish. One needs a shortwave radio to receive BBC or the Voice of America.

Satellite television has increased greatly since the 1990s. Even in poorer neighborhoods, satellite dishes can be seen everywhere. Popular channels include the Egyptian and French channels along with *Al-Jazeera*, a Qatari-based news and current affairs channel that started up when the BBC's

Arabic TV service closed. *Arte*, the Franco-German arts channel, has a loyal following. Also there are now four Tunisian satellite channels, two state-run and two private.

For Tunisians without satellite television, the TV fare is very limited. In Arabic, there is Channel 7, which broadcasts news, Egyptian films and soap operas, sporting events, and documentaries dubbed into Arabic. Locally produced material is limited to a Saturday night variety show, *Mindhar* (a current affairs program), and a Ramadan soap opera. There is also RAI Uno, the main Italian channel, and France 2, much watched for news and current affairs, which is rebroadcast in Tunisia. The sole domestic provider of broadcast content, for both radio and television, is the state-run company Etablissement de la Radiodiffusion Télévision Tunisienne (ERTT).

Press

The most important daily newspapers are the following: *Ach-Chourouk* (The Sunrise), the largest-circulation, independent, Arabic-language newspaper, which keeps its readers up-to-date with Tunisia's singers and soccer players; *As Sabah* (The Morning), an independent daily, with news stories and features from the Maghreb; *Le Renouveau* (The Renewal), the official organ of the ruling RCD Party; and *La Presse*, a government-owned, French-language newspaper that carries restaurant ads, tender notices, plane arrival and departure times, and a good literary page on Mondays. The bilingual Arabic–French weekly *Réalités* is the most respected magazine, covering political and economic news along with historical and cultural features. The weekly newspaper *Tunisia News* is the only locally published English-language periodical. The *International Herald Tribune* arrives in Tunis late on the day of publication.

SERVICES
Telephone

The telephone service is generally good. Most people have telephones in their homes, and there are public telephones in all towns and cities and in most villages under the name *Publitel* or *Taxiphone*. In cities, simply look around—there is at least one on every street. Cell phones are common among young urban Tunisians.

In 2001, local telephone codes were incorporated into the individual numbers. This

means you have to dial the entire eight-digit number when calling locally. Landline numbers start with 7, and cell phone numbers usually start with 98 or 21. All public telephones can be used for both national and international direct dialing. The international dialing code for Tunisia is +216. The outgoing international code is 00, to be followed by the relevant country code.

The cell phones of most European carriers function in Tunisia, although those of US and Australian companies sometimes do not.

Mail

The Tunisian postal service, known as the PTT, is slow but reliable. Letters to and from Europe take about a week, and further destinations somewhat longer. Posting your letter from a big city post office usually speeds up delivery. There is also a (more expensive) *Rapide Poste* service, with links to DHL and other international express services.

Mail can be received *post restante* at any Tunisian post office. It should be addressed clearly, with your family name in capitals, as follows: (Name), Poste Restante, PTT Central, City Name, Postcode, Tunisia. Ask the clerk to check under your given name if you think mail is missing. A small collection fee is due for each letter at pickup.

Internet

Internet access is expanding rapidly in Tunisia. Two major Internet service providers offer residential service, and now even small towns have cyber cafés.

Government censorship of the Internet is a reality in Tunisia. Web sites considered subversive or corrupting (politics or pornography) may be blocked, including the popular video-sharing websites YouTube and Dailymotion, and the social networking Web site Facebook. E-mail messages may be filtered, with some arriving empty or disappearing from the inbox after being opened.

CONCLUSION

On March 20, 2006, Tunisians celebrated fifty years of independence, with much to be proud of: 80 percent of Tunisians own their own homes, two-thirds are middle class, and universal primary education is a reality for both sexes. Life expectancy is seventy-four years, as compared with fifty years at independence, and the poverty rate has dropped to a remarkably low 6 percent. Tunisia has achieved sustained economic growth, with the annual rate of growth rarely dipping below 5 percent.

In sum, Tunisia has turned itself into a modern, progressive, and prosperous country in a region of the world more noted for instability and extremism. Tunisia has led the Arab world in reforms to advance the status of women in society, and has accorded priority to education and other social programs seldom seen in the developing world.

There have been setbacks. Unemployment, which officially stands at 14.2 percent, has been a continuing problem. Tunisia has invested heavily in education and a demographic peak is now hitting higher education and the job market. Providing jobs for these highly educated people represents a major challenge for the government.

Despite its socioeconomic gains, Tunisia has taken only small steps toward a democratic political system, and its human rights record is far from stellar. Confronting Tunisia is the ever-present challenge presented by Islamic fundamentalism—similar to the conflict in Turkey between those committed to preservation of the Ataturk secular state and those who seek to create an Islamic republic.

Given these strains, the question arises whether the modern and progressive Tunisia of reforms and openness to the world will survive. Or will the social reforms of the last half-century be swept away and Tunisia remolded into a more traditionalist Islamic society?

As in Turkey, a key battleground issue is the head scarf. Under the pressure of Islamists, the *hijab* has made its appearance in Tunisia, popularized in conservative Arab satellite TV broadcasts. This has prompted a strongly negative reaction from the government. President Ben Ali has strongly criticized "imported and uninvited" Middle Eastern customs that threaten to displace "traditional Tunisian attire, a symbol of an identity rooted in our history."

This *Kulturkampf* is not likely to be perceived by the average first-time visitor to Tunisia. What he or she is most likely to see is warm, open people who thirst after knowledge, work hard, help the poor, and respect other faiths and creeds.

Tunisians have seen for themselves the harm wrought by Islamist extremism in neighboring states and seem ill-inclined to repeat this experience at home. The most likely scenario for Tunisia is a continuation of the status quo.

The Tunisian people are friendly and hospitable. They value good relationships, they are loyal to their friends, and they welcome visitors. If you show them that you are interested in Tunisia and in its history, culture, and traditions, they will respond enthusiastically and give you an unforgettable introduction into this rich and fascinating culture.

Further Reading

Allman, James. *Social Mobility, Education, and Development in Tunisia.* Leiden: Brill, 1979.

Braudel, Fernand. *The Mediterranean World in the Age of Philip II.* 2 vols. New York: Harper and Row, 1973.

Broughton, T.R.S. *The Romanization of Africa Proconsularis.* Baltimore: Johns Hopkins University Press, 1929.

Brown, Carl L. *The Tunisia of Ahmad Bey, 1837-1855.* Princeton, New Jersey: Princeton University Press, 1974.

Charles-Picard, Colette and Gilbert. *Life and Death of Carthage: A Survey of Punic History and Culture From Its Birth to the Final Tragedy.* New York: Taplinger, 1969.

Flaubert, Gustave. *Salammbo.* New York: Penguin Books, 1977.

Geyer, Georgie Anne. *Tunisia: A Journey Through A Country That Works.* London: Stacey International, 2003.

Khair al-Din al-Tunisi. *The Surest Path.* Cambridge, Massachusetts: Harvard University Press, 1967.

Moore, Clement Henry. *Tunisia Since Independence: The Dynamics of One-Party Government.* Westport, Connecticut: Greenwood Press, 1982.

Perkins, Kenneth J. *Tunisia: Crossroads of the Islamic and European Worlds.* Boulder, Colorado: Westview Press, 1986.

Perkins, Kenneth J. *A History of Modern Tunisia.* Cambridge: Cambridge University Press, 2004.

Rogerson, Barnaby. *A Traveler's History of North Africa.* Northampton, Massachusetts: Interlink Publishing, 1999.

Salem, Norma. *Habib Bourguiba, Islam, and the Creation of Tunisia.* London: Croom Helm, 1984.

Yetiv, Isaac. *1001 Proverbs From Tunisia.* Washington D.C.: Three Continents Press, 1987.

Zartman, William. *Tunisia: The Political Economy of Reform.* Boulder, Colorado: L. Rienner, 1991.

Ziadeh, Nicola. *Origins of Nationalism in Tunisia.* Beirut: American University of Beirut Press, 1962.

Complete Arabic: The Basics. New York: Living Language, 2005.

In-Flight Arabic. New York: Living Language, 2001.

USEFUL WEB SITES

Access Tunisia (www.access-Tunisia.com) A handy portal with excellent links.

Tunis Post (www.tunispost.com) A portal for international news sites with uncensored Tunisia stories.

Tunisia Guide (www.tunisiaguide.com) A US Tunisia Tourist Office Web site, with cultural and travel information.

Tunisia Online (www.tunisiaonline.com) A government-run site with good sections on the environment, women, history, and tourism, and Tunisian news in English, French, and Arabic.

Index

culture smart! tunisia